Creating With Your Thoughts

Jeremy Lopez

Creating With Your Thoughts

By Dr. Jeremy Lopez

Copyright © 2018 by Jeremy Lopez

Published by Identity Network

P.O. Box 383213

Birmingham, Alabama 35238

ENDORSEMENTS

"Within 'Creating With Your Thoughts,' Jeremy dives deep into the power of consciousness and shows us that we can create a world where the champion within us can shine and how we can manifest our desires to live a life of fulfillment. A must read!" – Greg S. Reid – Forbes and *Inc.* top-rated Keynote Speaker

"You are put on this earth with incredible potential and a divine destiny. This powerful, practical man shows you how to tap into powers you didn't even know you had." – Brian Tracy – Author, *The Power of Self Confidence*

"He has drawn from the wells of his prophetic anointing very insightful revelation for us today. Securing the reader in a fortress of truth. Making those who chose to walk in these spirit life principles stand taller and speak clearer about their God chosen destiny." – Roberts Liardon

"It is a transformational book that challenges you to rethink what you have been taught while reflecting ore deeply upon the truth you have come to know. The journey through this book is prophetic, mystical, and magical, as you come to know who you really are for all eternity." – Robert Ricciardelli

TABLE OF CONTENTS

FOREWORD

You are, both, powerful and eternal beyond belief. If you could learn to but see the limitless, pure and unadulterated potentiality which you truly do possess, never again will your life be the same. In an instant, the old will be wiped away and all things will become new. Creation is, in no uncertain terms, a very transformational process of renewal – moment by moment and day by day. When speaking of the Law of Creation, I would be remiss if I did not say that it is, first and foremost, a journey – a journey unending, as we begin to access not only the greater, hidden recesses of the power of the Divine Mind which we truly do possess but also the eternal essence of our own spiritual identity as Creator.

This limitless and abounding adventure of creation has literally everything to do with who we are as eternal spirits having a physical, human experience here within the earth realm. When writing my most recent book, *The Universe Is At Your Command: Vibrating the Creative Side of God*, I came to be reminded, even more so, the immense and vast power of the role our thoughts play within the creation process. Since the release of the book, I have received countless thousands upon thousands of responses from readers, just like you, throughout the world, asking about the pivotal next steps. "What happens next?" "After I recognize my power, then what?"

My friend, I have been quite literally overwhelmed by the response and have been so inspired to see, firsthand, the hunger of awakening now beginning to be ignited within humanity, once again – a hunger for the greater truths and the deeper mysteries of the Divine Mind which we truly do possess, which controls all things around us. Though I have been so very privileged to speak prophetically into the lives of millions throughout these past three decades, never before have I seen the awakening of the inner hunger of humanity the way I do today. Like never before, individuals, just like you, are beginning to be inspired, again, to begin to tap into the true and limitless power of the creative force which they have always innately possessed – taking control of their lives and their destinies, finally, just as the Godhead intended from the very beginning, as man was shaped from the very dust of the earth and as the very breath of creation's force animated him, all those years ago.

Now, though, as never before, as I find the world now inundated with the greater awakening of the truth of the Law of Attraction and the Law of Creation, I so often see various teachings which seem to leave out very vital, key elements of the creation process. Is the power of creation merely a process of visualization? Is it the thought which creates? If so, as some suggest, then what role do we, as people, play within the process? Are we merely the slaves of thoughts? Absolutely not.

Never once have we been apart from the creation process. I feel compelled, my dear friend, to write to you once again to share with you the rest of the story – other key and vital aspects of the creation process. My sincere hope and prayer is that you, beginning today, will not only be reminded of your own role within the creation process but that you will, again, be reminded of your eternal identity. As "He" is, so are you. You always have been. You always will be.

Illumination

All of creation began with a well-intentioned thought of illumination. With a thought of focused, harnessed intent, the Godhead – the Sovereign – stretched Himself across the expansive, empty nothingness and exhaled His very breath. It was this breath – this *ruach* – which would also come to animate the newly formed, freshly-shaped figure which had been molded from the clay of the ground beneath. However, the story first began with a great and forceful burst of light. In an instant, light burst ever-so forcefully throughout the cosmos, continually expanding so very quickly that the darkness, itself, could not keep pace. "Let there be light." Indeed, in an instant, there *was* light. It never ended. It still has yet to cease. The darkness found itself not only unable to keep pace with the speed of this great light, but it found itself unable to understand it, also. "And the light shineth in darkness; and the darkness comprehended it not." (John 1:5)

When speaking of this great light, it is important to realize, also, that its very existence is forever tied to the role of humanity. The annals of history, itself, are filled with vast imagery of "light" versus "darkness," often used by some to depict the war being waged between "good" and "evil." As a fan of history and philosophy, I find often find it quite interesting that, even within the historical context, entire periods of time within civilization were often characterized by the concepts of "light" versus "darkness." It was the Italian scholar Petrarch, in the 1330s, who originated the term "Dark Age," from the Latin *saeculum obscurum*, denoting a period of history which seemed so, so very tumultuous. Then, the *Renaissance* – the "rebirth" - came, followed by a period that is referred to as the "Age of Enlightenment," during the eighteenth century. Although these periods of time are often used to denote periods within which humanity shunned reason and intellect for superstition and religious dogma,

3

for many of us within humanity, it seems as though the "Dark Ages" never truly left, unfortunately.

We so fear even the usage of the term "enlightenment." To many, the word seems far too mystical or "new age." My friend, there is absolutely nothing more Biblically sound and theologically accurate than the concept of "enlightenment." In fact, Jesus, himself, often spoke in terms of "light," even comparing humanity to the "light" of the world. "Ye are the light of the world. A city that is set on a hill cannot be hid. Neither do men light a candle, and put it under a bushel, but on a candlestick; and it giveth light unto all that are in the house.

4

Let your light so shine before men, that they may see you good works and glorify your Father which is in heaven." (Matthew 5:14-16) My friend, the scriptures are filled, continuously with the imagery of light and illumination. In fact, the psalmist said, "Thy word is a lamp unto my feet, and a light unto my path." (Psalm 119:105)

Illumination, in a spiritual sense, refers, to the process of becoming awakened to the greater truths of the universe. This is, in no uncertain terms, the entire purpose of the Kingdom within which Jesus continually spoke of. I so often hear so many well-intentioned believers speak of "enlightenment" in terms that

5

seem very impractical and unattainable. However, my friend, the truth of the matter is that enlightenment – spiritual awakening – is the most natural process of all creation and the most vital. How can one fully begin to operate in the full measure of truth and power until first becoming awakened or "illuminated" to the reality of that power?

We must come to a place of not only recognition of truth but also to the point of understanding also, so that we may begin to incorporate the principles of truth into our daily lives and put them into practice. "And ye shall *know* the truth, and the truth shall make you free." (John 8:32) This passage of scripture, perhaps more so than any other, depicts Jesus speaking of enlightenment in His own words. Truth, in and of itself, is powerless and has no ability to free anyone. It isn't the truth that makes you free; it's the truth you *know* – the truth you are enlightened or illuminated to which frees you. For all of us, myself included, there are times and certain moments and seasons in which we are blinded. In fact, let's face it. We all, at times, have "blind spots." Let's look at this in a much more practical way, shall we? Think of the accidents which occur on our roadways each day because of "blind spots." Have you ever been driving, minding your own business, careful to pay attention to every movement and every turn when, suddenly and seemingly out of the blue, another vehicle roars past you and you didn't even see it coming?

Often times, there are "blind spots." So very often, in life, as we're moving the vehicle – the body – we are often taken by surprise because of things we simply do not see coming. The unexpected happens. Sharp turns occur, which cause us to seemingly, for a moment, lose our balance and our sense of Self. This, my friend, is why the prophetic voice is so very vital in the earth today. Contrary to what the darkness of religion teaches, it is not only possible to know what is coming up, but it is absolutely critical that we do. "The eyes of your understanding being **enlightened**; that ye may

know what is the hope of his calling." (Ephesians 1:18) In 1 Peter 5:8, we are admonished to be sober and to be vigilant. To be "sober" literally means to be "right-minded" and "alert."

When beginning to understand the creative power which we truly possess, it is vital that we be in our right minds and alert – awakened and illuminated to the truth of who we are. My friend, when you are illuminated and enlightened to the hope of your calling, you will begin to finally **see** past the "blind spots" of old paradigms and old patterns of thinking which have caused you to be hindered from walking into your true freedom. So very much is often sad about the "calling." We hear it practically every day in some regards. However, my friend, have you ever fully taken the time to simply ask, "What is hope of the calling?" In other words, what are we truly called to do?

As we think of how the Godhead illuminated the cosmos, when He envisioned us and the Divine calling which would inundate our very being, have you ever taken time to ask, "What did He truly want from us?" It's a rather simple and elementary question; however, in truth, the answer to the question is the most transcendent truth of all. "What does God want from us?" Make it personal. Ask, "What does

God want from *me?*" Did God create humanity – decree that the eternal souls already living within His presence would have an earthly experience – in order to simply have blind and forgetful followers who would simply float along through the earth realm without ever really having a say in the matter? If so, then how very illogical of Him. No, my friend, the Godhead is much more transcendent than that – the reality of the Spirit is far too vast and calculating.

The transcendent truth of the matter is that you were placed here within this earth realm with more of a say and more of a choice in the matter than what religion could ever describe. You are here to enact the Law of Creation, just as He, Himself, continues to do. More so, you are here to actually *know* His plan. I must admit, I so very often find it comical to hear teachers of the scriptures speak of the great mysteries as if we're somehow destined to never know the truth of existence as long as we're here – insinuating in some way that we're just here to blindly and forgetfully get by and hope that it all works out. What a shallow existence, my friend.

Contrary to what you've been taught and contrary to what many may continue to attempt to teach you, you are here with power to create and you have the absolute ability to *know*, beyond the shadow of a doubt, the will, the purpose, and the plan of God for your daily life. You have the power, even now, to know the destiny of God for yourself. In fact, the truth of the matter is that you are, even right now, much, much more in alignment with your destiny than it might seem, at first glance.

The Christian mystic, Meister Eckhart, famously said, "The eye through which I see God is the same eye through which God sees me; my eye and God's eye are one eye, one seeing, one knowing, one love." How very beautiful. How very true. I so very often hear, as perhaps you have, so many asking, "What is the will of God for my life?" Each day, I receive into the offices of Identity Network countless thousands upon thousands of requests for prophetic words from beautiful souls asking this same question. It's humbling, really. In truth, I so often find myself overwhelmed at the thought of just how truly humbling it is to know the mind of the Spirit and, even more so, to encourage others to recognize that they, too, possess the same Divine Mind of creation's power within themselves. In truth, that's what prophecy is, really. It is the thrust of the soul into the deeper truths of God – the moment at which the soul is awakened and illuminated by the truth of the Spirit.

When someone reaches out to me and inquires of the Spirit for their lives, I am not showing them something that they themselves cannot find. No, in fact, I am simply reminding them, by the power of the Spirit, who they truly are. This is why the power of prophecy is so vital and important. It awakens humanity to the truth. This is where success comes from. This is where awakening comes from. This is where empowerment comes from. It comes the instant the soul is awakened – illuminated and recalibrated – to the truth of the Spirit, in order for it to fully begin to manifest with its own creative power. I must admit, often, I find myself in amazement when someone comes to me to inquire of the Lord for their lives and I hear the voice of the Spirit respond to them, saying, simply, "Well, what do *you* want?" It's amazing really, just how truly incomprehensible our eternal oneness is with God. As I said in my book, *The Universe is at Your Command*, "You are one with God. You always have been. You always will be." There is no denying this truth, and it is this truth that is paramount to beginning to understand the role our thoughts play within the creation process.

When speaking of the Law of Creation, it is literally no exaggeration to suggest that our thoughts, quite literally, *are* His thoughts. This truth is, in itself, why thoughts become things. We are creators, just as our Father is. We have within us the same DNA of the Spirit, even now coursing through our veins – an internal, creative thrust of power which has the potency to speak things into existence, frame worlds and create galaxies, at will. Yes, this is the very real Law of Creation, and just as gravity brings back to the earth all that rises above its surface, within its atmosphere, so, too, is there no escaping the Law of Creation. My heart's cry is that you, as a powerful thinking and speaking spirit, would finally begin to realize just how very important your thoughts are and, even more so, begin to fully awaken to the continuous and eternal dynamics of the Divine Mind always at work. Truly, as "He" is, so are we.

I can still so very vividly remember once giving a prophetic word to a hungry, young soul who had come to me to inquire of the Lord. He said, "Jeremy, I find myself in a career that I literally hate. Each day I go to work I feel like I'm literally being drained of my life, in an environment that I absolutely despise." He went on to say, "I'm not being honored." He asked, "Is this really the will of God for my life?" The answer, of course, was, "No." I'll never forget the instant peace that seemed to all of the sudden come upon him. His countenance changed. A look of pain and depression was immediately replaced, almost instantaneously with an expression of joy and, most of all, freedom. However, he had already known this to be the answer; he simply hadn't allowed himself to awaken to the truth of the answer. In truth, his very own soul had known the entire time. So often, I'm asked why I choose to minister and teach upon the subject of the Law of Creation, and the answer is quite simple, really: "It's the essence of the Kingdom of God." In reality, there is absolutely nothing more integral to the awakening of the inner Kingdom of God within, which Jesus spoke of so often, than the reality of the creative power which we possess.

By awakening – by becoming enlightened to the truth of the Kingdom of God *within*, that is – we begin to step into the full measure of the creative power of God. Upon so doing, we find that, ironically, His power has always been our very own power all along. The young man would later write me and explain how he never could have even imagined being as content and satisfied as he had become after finally stepping out on faith to begin his own business. He explained, "I was working in that former job because my father had worked there. It was a family business and, although I never felt drawn to it, I worked there out of obligation." You see, my friend, as well-intentioned as he was and as sincere as he had been, he had allowed a "blind spot" – even the "blind spots" of others – to keep him trapped in an old paradigm of thinking, rather than stepping into his freedom. This occurrence is all too common and too familiar, in fact. I hear it so very often. In fact, if I may be completely transparent with you, I've often experienced it within my very own life.

Years ago, I would so often hear other ministers say, "Jeremy, are you sure you're supposed to step into the role of the prophetic and begin your own outreach?" Others would say, "Jeremy, are you sure this is the will of God for your life?" My friend, if I had not surrendered to my own, inner voice – the voice of the Spirit within me – the books would have never been written, the prophetic words would have never been delivered around the world, and

Identity Network would never have been privileged to take the gospel of Jesus Christ around the world. Sure, it would have been easy to continue ministering in my own, local community; however, I *knew* early on that the Spirit was calling me to step out into a much larger field. If I had not been "enlightened" to the hope of my calling, as Paul encouraged the church at Ephesus to be, I never would have begun to fulfill the calling upon my life. There would be no Identity Network had I not been able to *see* the truth of the plan of the Spirit for my own life. This, my dear friend, is my humble and sincere prayer for you in all areas of your life, and, as I write these words to you, it is the cry of my heart for all humanity:

illumination. In the Old Testament, Isaiah the prophet spoke concerning the coming age of the Kingdom, "The people that walked in darkness have seen a great light: they that dwell in the land of the shadow of death, upon them hath the light shined." (Isaiah 9:2) He was speaking, prophetically, not only of the coming Age of the Kingdom which we even now find ourselves living within but, even more so, of the Age of the Spirit.

From atop Sinai through centuries of religious legalism and dead "works," humanity had only been given a dark and shadowy analogy of the nature of God. Truly, the earth saw through a glass "darkly," even then.

However, when Jesus came, he uttered a simple truth that not only revolutionized man's understanding of the Spirit world; his was a truth that also revolutionized man's understanding of himself. "God is Spirit." (John 4:24)   From the very beginning, from the instant that the light had first come, up until the time when Jesus had spoken those words, humanity had been able to see only religious archetypes – we knew of nothing else, really. However, when we were told of spiritual truth, our hunger was satisfied.   By uttering his transcendent words, Jesus painted an image not of a violent and wrathful God who was so distant, isolated, lonely, and disconnected from the creation He had envisioned but, rather, as

24

the very energy behind it all – the force continuously operating behind the scenes at all times. Spirit is a very transcendent and often elusive concept to so, so many. Quite simply, my friend, Spirit is the driving force behind it all. Every breath. Every desire. Every intent. Every movement. "For in him we live, and move, and have our being; as certain also of your own ports have said, For we are also his offspring." (Acts 17:28) The very same breath which first exhaled the words which ushered the command, "Let there be light," was, in truth, the same breath which had caused animated life to come to the body of man within the garden.

It was the same rushing wind which would, then, ignite the church upon the Day of Pentecost. It is the breath within your own lungs, even now as you breathe. I want you to, for a moment, inhale very deeply as you read these words. Do you feel that? That inner vibration? That creative power? Yes, it is, indeed, the very same breath which was first breathed within the garden. All of history has, both, risen and fallen upon one, single breath. It is the breath of the Creator. As you breathe, you are manifesting His creative power.

Just As He Is

It's been said many times before that imitation is the most sincere form of flattery. In our culture in this modern society, those of prominence – notable public figures are often imitated, copied, parodied, and mimicked by those who would be like them. In fact, in all honesty, many times it is this imitation that confirms someone had attained a certain level of notoriety. From the latest fashion trends and styles to even certain mannerisms and vocal inflections, it seems that so very often many attempt to copy others. Throughout the years, in my line of work, I've been privileged to deliver prophetic readings to various celebrities of the stage and screen and also to those who work within the fashion industry. Although, most often, many of these notable and recognizable celebrities wish to remain anonymous for purposes of their own privacy, suffice it to say that celebrities really are just like us. They encounter the same pain, the same hardships, and, yes, even have the same questions about their love lives. Above all, just like us, they have a deep hunger for purpose and meaning. "What is my purpose?" "Why am I here?"

I remember speaking to a young woman once who, at the time, had just broken into the music industry. Growing up in a Christian home, she still found herself in search of the voice of the Spirit, even after having finally attained a certain level of success. I'll never forget, she said, "Jeremy, my work is constantly being copied and I don't know how to feel about it." I responded, "Well first of all, you should be flattered. Imitation is a form of flattery." If you've followed my work throughout the years, you know that for me, my true hero has always been and will always be my father, Jim Lopez. As far as I'm concerned, there will never be a more Godly, humble, or wise man that will ever walk this planet again. I'm sure other sons feel this way about their fathers, as well. However, for me, my father was not only influential in my life; he will forever be influential in my ministry and in my prophetic work, as well. Even now, I still sense his presence around me and I know he's always near me. Needless to say, I'm a very proud son. Proud, in fact, of both of my parents.

I've often spoke in the past of the importance of learning to "merge" the two worlds – that of the physical with that of the spiritual. Recognizing this important element is critical when speaking of the Law of Creation and learning to master the process of creating with your thoughts. In fact, this merging, as it were, is paramount to the process because it ties directly into the element of Oneness. The Divine Mind is a mind of Divine Union. Oh, hear me, my friend, when I say to you that there is truly no distance or separation in the world of the Spirit. You might ask why I began this chapter speaking to you about the issue of imitation and flattery and ask, "Jeremy, what does that have to do with mastering the power of my thought life?" Well, my friend, although the Godhead cares absolutely nothing about flattery, the Divine Mind loves absolutely nothing more than the act of obedience. In fact, obedience is greater than sacrifice. "And Samuel said, Hath the LORD as great delight in burnt offerings and sacrifices, as in obeying the voice of the LORD? Behold, to obey is better than sacrifice, and to hearken than the fat of rams." (1 Samuel 15:22) In this passage, the

Prophet Samuel defines perfectly the importance of not only spiritual discernment – hearing the voice of the Spirit – but most of all the importance of obedience.

You may still be asking, "Yes, but what does this have to do with imitation?" "Herein is our love made perfect, that we may have boldness in the day of judgment: because as he is, so are we in this world." (1 John 4:17) In John 10:30, Jesus says, quite emphatically, "I and my Father are one." In fact, in John 5:19, we see this principle of obedience shown even more remarkably. "Then answered Jesus and said unto them, Verily, verily, I say unto you. The Son can do *nothing* of himself, but what he seeth the Father do: for what things soever he doeth, these also doeth the Son likewise." In other words, Jesus did only what he saw the Father doing. John 5:20 continues, "For the Father loveth the Son and sheweth him all things that himself doeth: and he will shew him greater works than these, that ye may marvel." Oh, how I wish that you could receive this revelatory and transcendent truth! Do you want to truly *obey* God? Do you truly wish to manifest the will of God within the earth realm? Then *be* Him. Obey Him by *imitating* Him within the earth.

The obedience that the Lord delights in is imitation here and now! The imitation doesn't end there, however. Furthermore, Jesus went on to say that not only did he *see* what the Father was doing, but he also *heard* what the Father was doing. "Henceforth I call you not servants; for the servant knoweth not what his lord doeth: but I have called you friends; for *all things* that I have *heard* of my Father I have made known unto you." (John 15:15) Jesus also said, when concerning his own words, that his words were the very words of the Spirit flowing through him. "It is the spirit that quickeneth; the flesh profiteth nothing: the words that I speak unto you, they are spirit, and they are life." (John 6:63) How incredible to see the truth of the Oneness we share with the Godhead and with the Divine Mind. Imagine being so very in-tune, so very in-sync with the mind of the Spirit that never once would you ever again question, "Is this the will of God for my life?" "Should I do this?" "Is this the job for me?" "Is this the relationship I should have?" Well, my friend, as unbelievable as it may seem and as much as it baffles the religious mind to accept, you *are* this in-sync with the Divine Mind even now, as you read these words. Begin to walk in this truth and in this revelation. Accept it and embrace it.

Start to enact this identity, beginning today. Even now, within your own sphere of existence, my friend, begin to kill and to put to death the mindset which continually seeks to cause you to feel separate from God. The truth of the matter is that you could not even begin to be outside or separate or apart of disconnected for the will of God even if you wished to be. Why? Because you are one with God. When I first realized this powerful truth contained within scripture, not only did it change my life, but it also changed my access to the supernatural realm.

My friend, may I share with you a very powerful truth which religion simply does not want you to know about? It isn't blasphemous and it isn't sin to consider yourself one with God. The truth of the matter is, the only real blasphemy is when you do not. You are, even now, the living, breathing embodiment of the Divine Mind of God within the earth realm – the personification of the Godhead. There is no separating you from the totality of all that God is. Never for one moment allow religion to cheat you out of knowing the truth of your identity in the Spirit. Once you lay hold to the truth of your identity, hold onto it for dear life – cling to it, for it is priceless.

I'll never forget when I first became awakened to this powerful truth of Oneness in the early, beginning days of my ministry. Not only did it change my meditation and my prayer life, but it literally opened the portals of Heaven all around me. The miraculous became the

norm and, almost instantly, it seemed, the
supernatural power of the Spirit became a much
more evidential part of my work and ministry. I
began to *know* things about those I encountered.
The gift of prophecy already at work within my
life became so much more heightened and finely
tuned. I began to *hear* the voice of the Spirit
much more clearly, often as what could only be
described as audible. I began to *see* into the
deeper dimensions of the Spirit in ways that I
didn't even know were possible. Why? The
answer is quite simple. I AM one with God. I
AM one with the Divine Mind of the Spirit.
What He does, I do. What He says, I say. What
He hears, I hear. He reveals it to me. My
friend, the same power is available for you, even

now in your daily life and can be accessed the very moment that you simply recognize your true identity in the Spirit.

Recognizing this truth of the Oneness with God is absolutely the beginning of learning to master the creative power of thoughts. Did you know that the Spirit is wanting to be known in the earth? It's true. In fact, from the very beginning He has attempted to make Himself known to humanity, here within the earth realm. The moment that you begin to see the eternal connection which has always existed with the Spirit, I promise you, my friend, the supernatural will begin to become merely natural. The extraordinary will begin to become merely the ordinary. The miraculous will begin to become like second nature to you. In fact, the nature of the Spirit is our true nature. Never be deceived into believing that this physical plane of existence is all there is. Not only is this world of physical matter not even a fraction of all that exists, the truth is that it is only a projection of the powerful thoughts we are constantly creating with.

As I shared in my book *The Universe is at Your Command*, you are a powerful, thinking spirit – Divine in every way. My friend, may I share with you a very shocking truth? You are not a human being here to try to find some spiritual experience. No, you are a spiritual being here to enjoy a human experience. The physicality of this world, with its limitations, its heaviness and its dense matter, is in no way comparable to the totality of the unseen, spiritual world. When you begin to enact your true identity, imitating God within the earth *as* Him - then in an instant the unseen world will become visible to you. The shift begins within the mind.

Are you ready to begin to journey even more deeper into the vast terrain of the Spirit? Are you truly ready to begin witnessing the supernatural in your own, daily life? Stirring up the inner gift of prophecy within you and continuously rekindling the burning fire of the

Spirit within? You can begin to do just that the moment you begin to act as God acts here within the earth realm. For me, so often now as I'm delivering prophetic words to individuals, I find myself literally taken away, it seems, the imagery and the pictures being shown to me within my mind's eye seems so real. That's because it is real. In fact, it is more real than the physical world I now find myself living within.

I'll share much more about accessing the supernatural realm soon, and if you are interested in learning more about the power of prophecy, I encourage you to study my *School of the Prophets* course, available through Identity Network. However, concerning accessing the supernatural realm, allow me to simply say now that spiritual beings have no choice but to operate in the spiritual realm – to imitate and to copy that which is seen, heard, and known by the Divine Mind. My friend, it isn't your second nature; it's your primary nature! This physical nature is the illusion! In this book, I will be sharing with you very revolutionary truths which you, perhaps, have never heard before and, in order for you to receive the greater truths into your spirit, you must first recognize this very simple truth at the very start: You are *one* with the Spirit. Think of, if you will, the Spirit as being the fabric behind all things that we see and also all things which we cannot see. After all, has it not been

43

written that Christ is in *all things*? After all, do the scriptures not teach that He is Lord of *all*? Doesn't *all* mean *all*?

If you are truly going to believe the Word of the Lord then you must settle, once and for all within your mind, there is absolutely no distance between you and God. In fact, when speaking of Oneness, it is important that we even remove the word "between" from our vocabularies. There is no distance because, in truth, there aren't two identities. There is only one identity – that of the Spirit. "For by him were *all things* created, that are in heaven, and that are in earth, visible and invisible, whether they be thrones, or dominions, or principalities, or powers: all things were created by him, and for him: And He is before all things, and in Him all things hold together." (Colossians 1:16-17) It cannot be made any more simply, my friend. It is the Spirit – the Divine Mind – who is literally "holding it all together." Every atom, every molecule, every cell, and every world contained within every galaxy – it is the Spirit. You and I are one with that Spirit.

Are you ready for an even more shocking revelation concerning your true identity? The identity that religion doesn't want you to know about? According to Colossians, Jesus was the literal image of the invisible God – the invisible Spirit. "Who is the image of the invisible God, the firstborn of every creature." (Colossians 1:15) When all of creation encountered Jesus, creation was witnessing, both, the image and the identity of God. And the same can be said of you and I. Yes, you read that correctly! The same can be said of you and I! In the story of creation, the Godhead uttered words that confirmed this truth. "Let us make man in our image." We are a race not of this world! We are *in* but not *of* this world.

My friend, we live in such a physical plane – a dense and heavy world filled with mass and matter. We're born into this earth after we incarnate into human flesh, and we become very forgetful. We forget that we were there with Him in the beginning – as Him. We then begin to feel so very disconnected and so very separate. As a result, we create worldwide religions, often in cult-like fashion, in order to attempt to reach our spiritual nature again. The religions only make matters worse, in truth, because they promote the false narrative of dualism and dichotomy – that there are two identities, rather than one, unified, spiritual identity.

Thankfully, though, then Jesus came. He reminded us of who we truly are and always had been. That we aren't some race of depraved, fallen souls, destined for doom simply because a man and a woman ate an apple. He removed the scales from our eyes and caused us to see again. He reminded us to look within. My friend, there is no church, no institution, no teacher, no prophet, no mystic, no denomination, no guru, no healer, no evangelist, no angel, or saint capable of doing for you what Jesus did. He showed us the way, and the way was inward – within – into the inner Kingdom of God. "The Kingdom of God is within you." (Luke 17:21) As Jesus uttered those words, everything changed. The blinded eyes were opened. The lame began to walk. Demons were cast out. All manner of sickness and disease was healed. And, remarkably, in uttering these words, he was giving all of humanity a glimpse into the behind-the-scenes mechanics of the miraculous – he was letting us all in on the secret to the power of creation. Just as had been shown and told by the Father, he was allowing us to recognize – reminding us – that we, too, possess the same great union.

Have you ever stopped to think for a moment that long before Jesus ever went to the cross, he was already telling the world that the Kingdom was within them? Think of that for a moment. You see, religion has it all backward. Jesus did not come to place the Kingdom of Heaven within you; he came to activate and to awaken the Kingdom of Heaven already there which we had forgotten about! The Pharisees hated him. The religious elite of that day literally despised him. So much, in fact, that they crucified him. Today, where religion is concerned, not much has changed, unfortunately. You know this to be true, just as I do. The religious world probably takes issue with you reading this book, if we were to be completely honest. I realized decades ago that the religious world will never fully accept me because of the power that I walk in. The truth is, however, it cannot deny the God nature within me. The prophecies speak for themselves. The miracles speak for themselves. The worldwide ministry speaks for itself. I say that not to boast or to speak with pride. No, I say that because I know the truth of my identity. I want, more than anything, for you to know your identity as well. When the religious Pharisees attack you for newfound power and your newfound truth, simply say to them that you're just imitating your Father.

Moving Beyond

Attraction

So much has been said throughout the years of the Law of Attraction, and rightfully so. I'm a firm believer in the power of the Law of Attraction. It's a universal principle and is just as much part of the Kingdom of God as any law of healing and the laws of prosperity. It's a fact. We are constantly attracting with our thoughts. I share much, much more about the principles of the Law of Attraction in my books *The Universe is at Your command* and *Power Attraction.* I've been asked throughout the years why I have placed such emphasis upon the power of the mind, and the truth is very simple. It is the realm of the Kingdom of God, within the earth realm. Also, I have a burning passion for individuals all throughout the world – for the whole of humanity – to awaken to its Divine power and purpose. I have a hunger to see the whole of the world awaken to its true identity as powerful spirit beings and begin to operate within the full measure of their Heavenly, spiritual inheritance. Also, quite simply, I just know that it works. I've seen it. I live the principles, daily, and see the results. Each day,

I awaken to the success found within these truths, and I want the same for your life.

I want you to be free from the grasp of limited thinking and lack and to step into the fullness of what God has for you. Each year, within the publishing industry, countless thousands upon thousands of books are released within the self-help and spirituality genres and tackle the subject of the Law of Attraction. As you well know, I've put out a few, myself, and I've been so truly humbled by the overwhelming response. Each and every day, I receive testimony after testimony of how the teaching has changed lives. I'm grateful for that. Truly. It matters to me. However, as I look at the self-help industry today and see so many teachings on the Law of Attraction, I can't help but feel that something is missing. Something seems to be lacking. To me, from my experience, it seems as though there are several key elements that have been overlooked in the most popular teachings. That is the purpose of this book. Is the Law of Attraction merely a process of wishful thinking and visualization, or is there something more? If you've followed my work for any amount of time, you know that I have shared the answer to that question many times before. There is much, much more.

There is a process. There is a process behind the mastering of the thoughts. It takes practice. It takes openness. Most of all, it takes a lot of patience and some trial and error, in all honesty. I've spent a lifetime perfecting a method that I know works 100% of the time, and this method of attracting, as well as others, are available exclusively through Identity Network in my books and schools of thought. However, after we realize that our thoughts are, truly, creating things, then what? Once we recognize the power and the universal importance of personal responsibility – that we are, in fact, creators of our lives – what next? Well, that question was, for me, part of the driving force behind the creation of this book. I made an agreement with the Spirit years ago in the very beginning days of my ministry in the prophetic that not only would I share the revelatory truths with the world but that I would, also, give detailed and practical advice on how to implement those truths into daily life.

So, now, after my most recent book, *The Universe is at Your Command*, here we are, once again moving into even greater depths of the mind. My friend, in order to fully master the Law of Attraction, you must realize that it is a principle forever linked and intrinsically interwoven with the Law of Creation. The Law of Attraction and the Law of Creation work hand in hand and always have. With each thought, you are not only attracting, but you are literally creating a new world around you – quite literally bending the energies of the universe to mold and to adjust to your decrees and desires. Just as the Godhead does. Did you know that it really isn't difficult to find the will of God for your life? It truly isn't. If you want to find the will of God for your life, begin by looking at your very own desires. Do you truly want to know what God wants for your life? If so, begin by learning to recognize what it is that you truly want. Want to know what the Spirit desires? Well, what do *you* desire? You have the DNA of Spirit at work within your life at all times – the eternal Oneness of the Divine Mind in operation within your daily life, with each and every thought and desire. Remember, my friend, that the Divine Mind of the Spirit doesn't suffer from schizophrenia or from bipolar disorder. There aren't two wills and two minds at work; there is only one mind, working through you! Not only is there only one mind, there is only one singular will. This is the essence of Oneness. The psalmist said, "Delight thyself also in the LORD; and he shall give thee the desires of thine heart." (Psalm 37:4) Have you ever taken the time to stop and think how this could possibly be? Have you ever found yourself asking, "Why?" Well, the truth of the matter isn't, simply, that the Godhead is attempting to show partiality, always looking for certain, select people who delight in Him so that He can bless only them. Let's examine that passage in this way: Because of our eternal Oneness with the Godhead, the desires within our hearts *are*, in fact, His very own desires! Remember, there is no distinction or separation. Oh, my friend, how I wish that you could receive this Divine truth! The psalmist described it in this manner: "But his delight is in the law of the Lord; and in his law doth he meditate day and night. And he shall be like a tree planted by the rivers of water, that bringeth forth his fruit in his season; his leaf also shall not wither; and whatsoever he doeth shall prosper." (Psalm 1:2-3) In this passage of scripture, the psalmist says, quite directly, that when the "law" of the Lord is "meditated" upon, continuously, that there will be prosperity. This outlines the Law of Creation at work, perhaps, more than any other passage of scripture! If one were to more closely examine this passage within the original language, one would find that the word "meditate" is actually described with the usage of the Hebrew word *jehgeh*, which implies a "deep and serious thoughtfulness." Another way to say this is that for those who possess a "deep and serious thoughtfulness" of the Law of Creation, the creative process becomes second nature – more than just an inclination.

The usage of the Hebrew wording within this context means, quite literally, "to bend" or "to reshape." In other words, your very focused thoughts are "bending" or "shaping" the world around you, literally creating the prosperity you seek. This is the Law of Creation at work. It is impossible to speak of the Law of Attraction without also speaking of the Law of Creation. The two are pivotally interwoven, and it is the thought which brings the two worlds into manifestation. So, in this book, I want to take you even deeper into the power of the creative force – deeper into the realm of the thought form. The Spirit, through Jesus, said that if He be lifted up, He would draw all men unto Himself. "And I, if I be lifted up from the earth, will draw all men unto me." (John 12:32) The word "draw" should quite literally be replaced

63

with "drag," as it is the more appropriate word in the original language. Quite literally, when you begin to focus upon your own thoughts and your own creative power, the Spirit is "dragging" to you all that you are decreeing! What invincible, otherworldly power!

The Divine Mind of the Spirit *is* the mind of Christ. There is no separation – no distinction. The Spirit moving through you, through your own desires, are the very thoughts of Christ being decreed in the earth realm and in the heavenly realm and in the spirit realm. In Philippians 2:5, the Apostle Paul admonishes, "Let this mind be in you, which was also in Christ Jesus." Notice that he didn't say the mind of Christ isn't already your own mind. He said "let it be." In other words, allow it to be. Oh, my friend, how very often have we failed to *allow* the Christ nature to be working within us? How often have we simply attempted to stop it with our own thoughts and ideas of separation? "This isn't what God wants," we say. We ask, "Is this the will of God?" "How can I possibly have *this* in my life?" Such thoughts are the antithesis of allowing. By thinking these thoughts, we aren't "letting" the mind of Christ work within us. After all, is this not the very essence of the gospel itself? The inner work of the Spirit, within? Within the mind? Within the thoughts? "To them God has chosen to make known among the Gentiles the glorious riches of this mystery, which is Christ *in* you, he hope of glory." (Colossians 1:27) My friend, shall I say it another way to more adequately explain? You *are* Christ. Philippians 2:6 declares, "Who, being in the *form* of God, thought it not robbery to be *equal* with God." My friend, it simply cannot be made any more plain. You are constantly creating with your thoughts and your very thoughts are the thoughts of God. Knowing now that the Law of Attraction and the Law of Creation are intrinsically interwoven, how very important is it that we harness out thoughts? It is vital!

Did you know that in each and every moment you are thinking and that with each thought you are literally being initiated into the act of creation? It's true. This is why our feelings and our emotions matter. This, too, is why it is so very, very vital that we be in touch with our emotions. Now, when is the last time you've heard a sermon preached about getting in touch with your emotions and feelings? The sad truth is that you rarely ever will. Why? Because, again, religion focuses upon the outward man rather than the reality of the inner Christ. It says, very emphatically, really, that it's impossible to truly know the plan of God and that our feelings and our wants and our desires are in some way sinful, depraved, and unlike the nature of God. This is why so many repress their emotions and their feelings, only to, at some point, suffer literal breakdowns emotionally. My friend, your wants matter. Your emotions matter. Your feelings matter. Your desires matter. Why? Because they are the thoughts, desires, feelings, and wants of God. Anyone who tells you otherwise is still living within the paradigm of the old covenant and not in the Spirit.

We are literally living in a new season, because of the reality of the Spirit which Jesus led us toward and awakened us to. Did you know that Jewish mystics view the term "God" not as a noun or as a subject, but, rather, as a verb and as a word of action and creative force? It's true. According to Rabbi David Cooper, as detailed in his teaching *GOD is a Verb*, "God is not a thing, a being, a noun. It does not exist, as existence is defined, for it takes up no space (or includes all space but is not limited by it) and is not bound by time. Jewish mystics often refer to it as *Ein Sof*, which means Endlessness. Imagine that, won't you? Doesn't that redefine and reshape the manmade ideas and concepts of God that have been instilled into us by religion throughout the centuries? What if we began to see God not as someone set on judgment but, rather, as the loving force of creation? So at one with us that His very breath and being are continuously being enacted through us in each moment? Imagine what the Pharisees would say about that? God is action and the thought behind the action. God is the movement and the emotion which inspires the movement. God is the dream and the destiny, both, simultaneously. Truly, He is above all things and is in all things.

I often like to use this analogy to describe the characteristics of God: "God is inside the box. God is outside the box. God is the box itself." If you've followed me for years, you've heard me say this on occasion. It's so true, though, if you think about it. How else can we even begin to describe an omnipotent and omnipresent Spirit? Our words fail us. Our terms are inadequate. They are meaningless when compared to the all-inclusive and expansive nature of the Godhead. He simply *is*.

And so are we. God is a movement and He is the motion, also. I share this with you, my friend, in hopes of helping you become unstuck in your thinking. When will you stop judging and condemning yourself for being who you are? Stop condemning your humanity by erroneously believing that it somehow diminishes your spirituality. How can you judge God? What audacity. What pride. What foolishness, if we really think about it. However, as outlandish as the comparison might seem to the religious mind, that is exactly what you are doing each and every time you even begin to think, "Should I want this?" The moment you read those words, chains just fell from you in the Spirit. I know this prophetically. The more you begin to meditate and to ponder – to think – of the creation power which resides within you, the more you will begin to become more firmly planted and rooted like a tree, as the psalmist described. God is a creative force which radiates throughout generations. The power of creation is your very divine birthright. Stop allowing religion to cheat you from embracing your true identity as the Creator.

I am absolutely convinced – I know – that the more we become aware of our creative power, the more we will begin to master our creations. We will begin to master our thoughts. In order to do this, however, some old thoughts have to die. Some new thoughts must be born. Old paradigms and old ways of thinking must be placed upon the altar of the Spirit and burned to ashes if you are ever going to step into the full measure of the power of creation. It can begin today, in an instant, the moment you begin to see just how loved and accepted you truly are. Stop judging your creation unfavorably, because by doing so you are only continuing to create more of the same. Like attracts like. My friend, it is a Divine principle of the Kingdom. What you think, you attract. What you think, you create. Your thought is your decree and your command to the universe.

I learned, years ago, the vast importance of mixing visualization and meditation with my prayers. For me, it was this powerful Law of Creation that not only birthed the dream which launched Identity Network, but it was also this practice and this universal Law of Creation which have taken the gospel numerous times all around the globe. I say this not to be proud or boastful but to, rather, say that I know from experience the power of the Law of Creation. Can I tell you something that may come as quite a shock, at first? I get everything and anything I want. I truly do. Why? Not because God blesses me in ways that He cannot bless you, but because I learned long ago that it is the Spirit within which is, both, attracting and creating the world around me that I desire. When I do not desire something, I've learned to simply put the thought out of my mind. You are, both, an attractor and a creator. I learned long ago that it is with the thoughts that we manifest the lives we truly desire. Oh, how I long for the whole of humanity to come to this understanding and to begin accessing their full potential.

I promise you, the very moment you begin to recognize your own creative power and the creative force behind the thoughts because of your covenant agreement with the Spirit, never again will you settle for the status-quo, mundane mediocrity of lifeless, cold, stale and dead religions which keep you feeling separated from God. In fact, you'll never be the same. The old mindset will simply not satisfy any longer. I feel that we are now living within a time in which we are hearing the final death rattles of religion – the institutions which seek to control and separate and manipulate the masses by using their tools of fear. Once you become free – once the truth is illuminated, never again will you ever be the same. The true church – His bride – is one of power and might and creative authority, capable of literally "bending" the energies of the universe to their demands and decrees.

Today, begin to boldly declare your true and authentic identity to the world around you.

Begin to decree into the atmosphere of your home, your job, and into your finances that you are a powerful creator and that the very Divine Mind which framed the worlds into existence in the very beginning is even now framing the world around you in your daily life. Begin to see yourself the way He sees you. He sees you the same way He sees Himself.

Beyond the Thought

We know now that thoughts become things. However, did you know that along with a creative and forceful burst of creative energy behind each thought also comes the triggering of feeling and emotion? We were designed, both physically and spiritually, to experience all of creation. Oh, how beautiful to know that we were designed to experience this wonderful life here on earth and all that comes with the human experience. The joys, the pains, the excitement, and the adventure – we were designed to experience it all. From the sound of a baby crying to the sound of your favorite song filling the air and from the taste of your favorite dish to the sights of your summer getaway, this life and all that it entails is meant to not only be experienced and enjoyed, but also processed.

As we've discussed in many of my other teachings, the brain is a very powerful and complex form within the human body capable of not only molding and shaping to enforce certain beliefs and ideas and feelings but also to cause us to feel even more of the same emotions which feel so very good. I speak much more about the topic of neural plasticity in my most recent book *The Universe is at Your Command,*

and in it I also discuss in great detail how with each thought new neural pathways are formed to propagate even more of the same thought. In other words, as shocking as it might seem, we are always creating more of the same. That is why it is so vitally important that we begin to be more aware of what it is that we are thinking, meditating and dwelling upon. Like attracts like. However, it is also important that we now begin to realize just how important a role our thoughts play in the process of creation. In fact, there is much to be said about this.

So very often, when listening to or reading other teachings concerning the power of the Law of Attraction, this, to me, always seems to be the key element that many other teachers haphazardly leave out when describing the creation process. In fact, I'm often asked, "Jeremy, if my thoughts are really creating my own reality, then what role am I playing in the process?" In other words, if it is the thought that becomes the *thing*, then what role, if any, are we to play during the creation process. This is often left unexplained by many who now currently teach the Law of Attraction, and, I must admit, I firmly believe that this is casually neglected or omitted from many popular teachings, quite simply, because many have yet to incorporate the Law of Creation into their lives properly, in-sync with the Law of

Attraction. Remember that both are pivotally interwoven into the fabric of all that is.

Well, my friend, allow me to share with you something even more transcendent: You are independent of the thought. In other words, shall I say it another way? You – the real *you* – are not the thought. You may now find yourself asking, "If I'm not the thought then what am I?" You are the "observer." Metaphysics explores the nature and the science behind all of the non-physical world. In fact, the term "meta," quite literally, means "beyond." When beginning to study the concepts of metaphysics and quantum mechanics, it is important to remember that we are studying that which is "beyond" the natural world. This includes, but is not limited to, the study of emotion, intuition, spirituality, quantum physics, physiology and all manner of non-physical phenomena. In reality, metaphysics is the study of what makes you – the real *you* – who you are. We're now living within a day in age in which science is even beginning to confirm that, just as Jesus said all those centuries ago, God truly is *Spirit.* My friend, I often find it unbelievable to see sincere individuals – men and women of sincere faith and belief – often shunning the study of science, thinking that science somehow negates spirituality. This is simply not the case. If anything, science is merely confirming the deeper mysteries contained within the scriptures.

The "observer effect" is a term used within the study of physics to describe a very real and very confirmable scientific truth: "Observing a situation or a phenomenon literally changes that situation or that phenomenon." Yes, you read that correctly. Please stay with me as we delve into these greater depths of the mind. You – the real *you* – are not the thought, you are the one "observing" the thought. According to Nikola Tesla, one of history's greatest scientific minds and also a great philosophical mind concerning unseen phenomena, the day science begins to study non-physical phenomena, it will make more progress in one decade than in all of the previous centuries of its existence." What a profound statement. Thankfully, we are now living in such an age in which the study of metaphysics and quantum mechanics is confirming, yet again, that there is, in fact, a very real unseen world just beyond natural sight which is continuously at work. You may ask, though, "Jeremy, what is the 'observer,' really?" My friend, as the Jewish mystics say, it is quite simply the "Endlessness." The "eternal."

I want you to do something. Right now, if you will, take a moment, even as you are reading these words, and right now envision a beautiful, lush field, filled with your favorite flowers. The sun is beaming in a lovely blue sky overhead. Are you doing it? Did you envision it? Well, of course you did. The truth of the matter is that envisioning such a place required very little effort on your part. It wasn't difficult to do, was it? In fact, it just came naturally. As you even read the words, the imagery followed – the internal imagery flooded your mind's eye. Almost as if you were watching a film play upon the screen of your mind, the images began to come. You saw the flowers. You might have even felt the grass beneath your feet. You were "observing" it. You were a witness. Well, my friend, the same concept applies to literally all thoughts – both the positive and welcomed and the negative and unwanted. All thoughts are viewed and observed. You are not your thoughts; you are the one watching as the thoughts come. This "observer effect" is, in many ways, a safeguard to the power of the creative process.

If the thoughts, themselves, were the actual creator then we would have so much unlimited chaos. Instead, rather, by the perfect plan of the Divine Mind, we are given the ability to see our thoughts – to look *behind* them – and to see what is really happening. To truly begin to truly master the process of creating with your thoughts, begin to look *behind* your thoughts, into the behind-the-scenes of it all.

We exist, as powerful thinking spirits, capable of filtering our thoughts. I know, at first glance, the idea of filtering your thoughts might seem to be a little overwhelming at first. So many thoughts so very often seem to spill onto the canvas of our mind so randomly throughout the day. It can often feel as if we have no control in the matter.

The truth is, however, that we are always able to choose which thoughts we hold onto and which thoughts we choose to shun. We possess the ability to censor, if you will, the creative process by being able to witness the thought as it appears in our minds. In other words, think of it this way. You, my friend, have been given a front row seat to the scenery of your life, and you are constantly being asked by the Spirit, "Do you want to keep this thought?" In his second epistle to the church at Corinth, Paul speaks of the power of censoring our thoughts. He says it this way: "Casting down imaginations, and every high thing that exalteth itself against the knowledge of God, and bringing into captivity every thought to the obedience of Christ." (2 Corinthians 10:5) To put it much more simply, we possess the Divine ability to censor our thoughts, constantly being able to compare them to the tapestry of the Divine Mind of the Spirit. In other words, though it may sometimes feel as though we have no control of what imagery flashes across the screens of our minds, we absolutely have a say in what we chose to give our full attention to. We have the power, the ability, and the Divine right to kill certain thoughts – to cast them down – and to replace them with other, much more positive thoughts.

"Finally, brethren, whatsoever things are true, whatsoever things are honest, whatsoever things are just, whatsoever things are pure, whatsoever things are lovely, whatsoever things are of good report; if there be any virtue, and if there be any praise, think on these things." (Philippians 4:8) Think of the good. Think of the beautiful. Think of the lovely and the positive. Although the power behind the Law of

Creation goes far, far beyond mere positive thinking, the truth is that there is much to be said of choosing to dwell on the good and forsake the bad. Because you are not your thoughts and you are, rather, the "observer" of your thoughts, you possess this Divine power.

Remember that like will always attract like. I remember once, years ago, while ministering in Hollywood, a young woman once approached me as I was leaving the coliseum and asked, "Jeremy, what do I do when a thought comes to my mind that I don't want to manifest? What do I do when a negative thought just 'pops' in there?" I replied, quite simply, "Just pay it no mind." Many ask, "Can it really be this simple?" The answer is "Yes." You see, my friend, it isn't the passing thought, itself that manifests; it is the thought we give place to – that we meditate upon and think intently upon – which manifests. In other words, the universe is always giving us a moment to rethink our thoughts!

We are always, in each and every moment, being given the opportunity to rethink the internal imagery constantly being flashed upon the screen of the mind's eye. Once, years ago, a woman who had recently had recently given birth to her first son spoke to me of how for months, after giving birth, she found herself continually facing fears which seemed to literally plague her mind. She recounted to me, in great detail, how literally each and every night she found herself wondering, "Is my baby breathing?" "Is he okay?" "Will something happen today that I won't be able to protect him from?" Of course, these are, in some ways, the very natural elements of the maternal instinct of protection. However, as she described to me, her fears were often very irrational and overwhelming.

She had just purchased her copy of the best-selling book *The Secret* and, rather than finding a sense of peace, she explained to me that she had, rather, found a sense of overwhelming dread. She thought, "Are these thoughts going to happen? Am I bringing danger to my child when these thoughts come to my mind?" The Spirit, through me, offered her assurance that I feel compelled to offer to you, also. I spoke to her and said, "Are your thoughts in alignment with your desire? If not, simply focus more upon your desire than upon your passing thoughts." You see, in no way was it her intention to bring harm or danger upon her newborn child; she simply had worry and fear which had begun to consume her.

As the very popular book seemed to suggest, her thoughts, themselves, were inevitably going to create havoc and bring disease or death upon her child, simply because of the images that continuously seemed to flash upon the screen of her mind. Did she want danger to come to her child? Of course not! So, for this reason, the Spirit simply encouraged her to focus more upon her true desire rather than upon the flashing imagery of her thoughts. In other words, her *true* desire was for her son to grow and become strong and healthy and to prosper and be safe. The Spirit encouraged her to begin to focus upon *that*, instead.

You see, my friend, it isn't the thought, itself, that manifests and creates; it is the thought that we give place to – that we focus intently upon – and that we make to partner with our true desires which manifests and creates.

There must be internal agreement. This is why it is so vitally and pivotally important – imperative, really – that we begin to look behind the thought and into the behind-the-scenes of the genuine intention. You see, for me, this is one of the main reasons why I felt inspired to offer this book to the world. It isn't in any way that the teaching of the Law of Attraction is incorrect; the issue is that other, important key elements are often left out of the teachings of others.

I want you to possess not only a proper and mature understanding of the Law of Creation but also have a true and working knowledge of just how to fully masterr it.

Again, you are not your thoughts. You – the powerful Spirit being within – are the one witnessing the thoughts. Go deeper. Go behind. Begin to peer behind each and every thought. Begin to analyze. Go into the deeper recesses of the mind and of the emotions to gain a better understanding of the Spirit within. Do you want to truly know God? Then begin to have a better, more mature and proper understanding of the Self.

As we've discussed before, thoughts create energy. In fact, the scriptures are replete with this creative force. From atop Sinai, the Lord caused his *Energeia* – his energy – to pass before the face of Moses, as detailed in Exodus chapter 33. Right now, today, you possess a power you have yet to fully comprehend. You, my friend, being the powerful and eternal spirit which you are, have been given a front row seat to the scenery of your life. You've been given the ability to witness – to "observe" – the thoughts you have, in real time. With each and every passing thought, the Divine Mind of the Spirit is continually asking, "Would you like to proceed?" "Would you like to manifest this?" As the question is asked, your feelings and emotions signal the way ahead. Does the thought feel good? Is it pleasant? Is it something you'd enjoy more of? Do you wish for the feeling to remain? If so, then meditate upon it – study it. If not, if it is an unpleasant thought, you possess the power kill it. Divert your attention and your focus to other thoughts. Replace the bad with the good.

I've lived by this principle since the beginning of my time in the prophetic ministry, and, not only do I know that it works, I've seen it work in the lives of countless thousands upon thousands of others. There is, even now, an energy of creation being enacted as you read these words. If you become sensitive to the moving of the Spirit, you will feel the presence of creation's power, even now, coursing through you – a vibration and a beckoning call of manifestation. So very often, I find myself even pressing the "pause" button upon the remote, allowing myself time to ponder the images of my thoughts and the future plans that they represent. I know, full well, that the choice to manifest it into reality or to refrain from manifesting it is entirely up to me and to me, alone. You possess this same ability, as an observer – as a witness. Did Jesus not say to his disciples, at the onset of the church, that they would be literal witnesses unto him? That they would be observers of the supernatural power which would soon inundate their very lives? As the fire of the Spirit burned ever-so brightly upon that first day – the birth of the church – creation was being enacted. In truth, prior to the fire falling, the disciples had been given time to ponder and to visualize what would soon come.

They waited patiently and rather anxiously for the manifestation. Then, it happened. A partnership from on high. The fire consumed them, initiating them into a realm of limitless possibility and pure potentiality. In an instant, it all became clear.

Gone were the days of patiently waiting in the dark – waiting for signs. They became emboldened and then, themselves, began to create. They turned the entire known world upside down with the power of creation's call after having been initiated into the fire of Pentecost. The Law of Creation, to them, became the very heartbeat of all that they would do for His name. As the fire feel upon them, it all made sense. I often think that as the burning embers of the Spirit became fanned into open flame that perhaps Peter was reminded of the words that Jesus had spoken only months prior. "God is Spirit." I often envision that, in an instant, he immediately became awakened to the truth of his own eternal Oneness. Today, as the Spirit's Divine Mind rises upon you, you are now being asked to simply remember. Remember the power you have. Remember the very selective power you possess to not only view the thoughts which flood your mind but also your own Divine ability to censor – to gauge the feeling behind your own creative force. This is the art of mastering creation. It is yours, even now.

An Inspired Life

There's an old adage about learning to view the world through rose-colored glasses that I've always found quite amusing. Not as amusing, though, as the question about seeing the glass half-empty or half-full. Whenever I've heard the question asked, I've always thought to myself, "Enjoy your juice. If you want more, get more. If not, then don't. Learn some responsibility!" Although I say that jokingly, the truth of the matter is that there is so much to always be said about the way that we choose to view things. Perception is such an important element of life that we sometimes miss it. In fact, while we're on the subject of witty sayings, I'm sure you've heard this one: "Don't miss the forest for the trees." It's a saying that implies it's often times so easy to miss what's right in front of us. It's true though.

Perception is such an intricately woven thread within the tapestry of existence that we sometimes never really take the time to actually see things for the way they truly are – we very rarely even take the time to observe. Whether we realize it or not, we are constantly, day in and day out, *filtering* the world around us through the lenses of our own, unique programming and conditioning. I *choose* to see the good, rather than the bad. I choose to see only the best. According to Romans 8:28, "And we *know* that *all things* work together for *good* to them that love God, to them who are called according to his purpose." Do we believe that? I mean, really? If all things are being made to work together for good, then why choose to dwell on the bad?

Now, I'm in no way suggesting that "bad" doesn't exist within the physical world of ours; I'm simply saying that we have the power to choose how we deal with it. Rather than living a life of negativity, my friend, make the choice to be inspired. Choose to live an inspired life. When we view the word "inspiration," we're actually viewing two words: "In-Spirit." Choose to be "In-Spirit," at all times. The words of the late Dr. Wayne W. Dyer, the brilliant author and philosopher, come to mind, as I write these words to you. In his book, *Inspiration: Your Ultimate Calling*, he says, "There's a voice in the Universe entreating us to remember our purpose, our reason for being here now in this world of impermanence. The voice whispers, shouts, and sings to us that this experience – of being in form, space, and time – has meaning. The voice belongs to inspiration, which is within each and every one of us." How very gorgeous. How very true.

We're always being drawn by the inner voice of inspiration toward a much more fulfilling life of Oneness – a life in which we recognize that there's a meaning behind literally everything that we see and also everything that we don't see. There's a greater, grander picture being painted at all times. Inspiration, I feel, is the force which causes us to begin to simply recognize the grander picture. I have a very dear friend who is a collector of art. He loves it, as do I. He once acquired a piece through an auction house in New York and wanted one of our mutual friends to view it as he proudly displayed it in his home for the first time. As the piece was unveiled, our friend looked at it in a rather puzzled way. It looked like such a mess. There were broad strokes across the canvas and colors that didn't seem to make any sense. It looked like such a messy piece of child's play, on the surface, at first glance. It was an abstract piece. Noticing the puzzled look upon our friend's face, the owner simply said, "Take a step back." When the "observer" finally took a step back, everything began to change, in an instant. Everything opened up. What, at first glance, appeared to be nothing more than messy lines and colors in disarray suddenly, in an instant, became a beautiful field and a bright blue skyline. Flowers began to emerge from the canvas. Deep blues and reds. It was so magnificent. You see, all that was required to see the beauty of the work was a simple shift of perspective. By taking a "step back," it all made sense. The picture became quite clear. It was a masterpiece that was worth every dime.

So very often in life, we miss out on the beauty, not because the beauty isn't there but because, from our vantage point, the beauty often comes to us in very messy ways. Like the divorce. Like the breakup. Like the loss of a job. Like the death of a loved one. At first glance, from our vantage point, the painting looks like nothing more than a series of splashes upon a canvas, without any rhyme or reason. It looks so very illogical. It sometimes feels even worse. Then, with time and practice – with patience – we learn to see from a new perspective. We learn to see the beauty. Everything begins to open up and we realize, finally, that there was a design all along. We see that there had always been a method to what once seemed like madness. Inspiration is a matter of perspective. Did you know that, contrary to popular belief and despite what most would say, it really is possible to be inspired each and every day of life? It's true!

My friend, I want to share with you a very important principle in learning to master the creation of your thoughts in this life: "Learn to move from separation into inspiration." Go beyond the feeling of separation and move into a realm of total inspiration. Move to the place "In-Spirit." Allow me to say it another way, won't you? Begin to move from the place of choosing to view the world around you as if it has no meaning and begin to view the world around you – your very own creation – as a world that has purpose in every minute detail. There was once a lovely young woman who came to Identity Network with questions about relationships. Her very long engagement had just come to an unexpected end only weeks prior and she found herself feeling completely alone. "Will I ever find love again?" "Am I destined to be alone forever?" Of course, in the overwhelming pain of a breakup these are natural feelings that we would all feel, momentarily. However, again, perspective is pivotal. I said to her, "Did you know that you can still enjoy your life, even now?" Now, as simple as that statement may seem, especially to someone in the throes of heartbreak and agonizing pain, it really is true. Allow me to explain. All of the experiences that she had wanted to enjoy with her partner were still there for her, still waiting to be experienced. I told her, "Take this time, in this season, to begin to enjoy your life like never before. Even if it feels like you have to force yourself to do it, at first. Enjoy delicious dinners. Attend the workshop. Treat yourself to the designer shoes. Go to see your favorite band perform live at the concert, even if you have to go alone." In other words, begin to experience, again, all that is out there just waiting to be experienced.

You see, my friend, so often, we allow the circumstances and the unexpected twists and turns of life to rob us from experiencing a full life. We allow these experiences – meant to be our teachers – to become our thieves, dead set on robbing us. Do not allow the circumstances of your life to rob you of your life experiences in this earth realm. We are here to not only enjoy this life, but we are here, by design, to absorb as many experiences as possible. This is why I so enjoy travel and dinner with my closest friends. It's because I'm determined to enjoy as many wonderful experiences here as possible.

Then, when I leave here one day, I'll continue to experience those things in the Spirit forever and ever!

This physical life – here – is just a passing phase, really. It's just a glimpse of a much grander picture – a larger design. The truth of the matter is, as unbelievably shocking as it might seem, you are never really alone. We are all connected. In fact, where relationships are concerned, Spirit has no gender. Yes, you read that correctly. Remember that like will always attract like. Focused intent upon the same will only create more of the same. If she had allowed the momentary pain of the breakup to cause her to become stuck in the feeling, she would have literally allowed the experience to rob her of other experiences. She would remain trapped. This is why I told her to step out again, even if she had to force herself to do it. Before long, she called to tell me some amazing news. "Jeremy, so much has changed in the past six weeks since I've been getting out more. There are three men who are showing interest in me, now! The thing is, though, as strange as it must seem, I'm really enjoying being single now!" You see, what had, after her breakup, seemed like such a devastating curse was, in fact, the beginning of one of the greatest seasons of her life. Stop waiting for people! Get out and begin to enjoy all the experiences that life has to offer!

Begin to be inspired – "In-Spirit." The dictionary defines the term "inspired" as "being imbued with the spirit to do something, by or as if divine or supernatural influence." Think of that for a moment. When we feel inspired, we are literally allowing the Spirit to begin to flow through us in Divine ways!

There are two passages of scripture which speak of inspiration being Divine. The passage in 2 Timothy 3:16 speaks of scripture being "inspired" by God, and 2 Peter 1:21 speaks of prophecy being "inspired" by the voice of God. The word "inspired" is actually a translation of the Greek word *theopneustos*, meaning, literally "God-breathed." Oh, that changes everything doesn't it? The Latin derivative of the word "inspiration" is *inspiare*, which literally means to "breathe upon" or to "blow into." Oh, my friend, how I wish that you would see this. Did you know that when the Godhead first formed man from the dust of the earth, the man was nothing more than a lifeless, dead, cold corpse until the breath of life was breathed into him? It wasn't until God breathed that breath that man then became animated and became a living soul. In other words, the man became "inspired" and began to come to life. Right now, my friend, you have perhaps gone through a very troubling season. My loving advice to you is to not allow it to take the wind out of your sails. Never allow the experiences of life to rob you from the pursuit of other experiences. Never allow your experiences to cause you to remain trapped in the moment of heartbreak.

Become inspired, today. Stop viewing yourself from the place of separation and disconnectedness and begin to recognize the masterpiece being painted all around you. You see, there is absolutely no distance in the Spirit realm. If you've just gone through a breakup or find yourself without a partner, begin to recognize that you are, even now, connected to literally everyone on earth, spiritually speaking. You aren't as alone as you'd like to believe you are. In fact, from the perspective of Spirit, you've never been alone. Not even once. This is why I teach that in order to begin to master the creation of our thoughts we must begin to move from the place of separation to the place of inspiration. We must begin to view ourselves as filled with the Spirit at all times, because, the truth of the matter is that we are.

As I've said before this physical world is the illusion. We are spiritual beings of the Divine Mind here within this earth realm to have a human experience. And can I share with you an even more life-changing revelation? We're supposed to enjoy it! We're supposed to enjoy our spirituality while also enjoying our humanity. As simple and as elementary as it might sound, my friend, your humanity doesn't separate you from God, regardless of what lies religion may have led you to believe. I know, according to the religious mind, we're all nothing more than just depraved sinners saved by God's grace and we'll never really amount to anything of substance, but that just isn't true. It's a lie. In fact, it's time you sent that idea of yourself back to the pits of "Hell" where it came from. There's a reason I place that term within quotations; however, that's another book for another time. I think of the "demonic" as literally anything that attempts to rob us from the experience of this life. After all, is that not what Jesus actually taught? That the purpose of the enemy is to rob us from life experiences?

Here's what I mean. "The thief cometh not, but for to steal, and to kill, and to destroy: I am come that they might have life, and that they might have it more abundantly." (John 10:10) Isn't it interesting that Jesus described the sole purpose of the thief as being to rob us of the fullness of life?

The thief isn't merely some archetypal "devil," my friend. The thief could be the unexpected situation or happenstance that you just haven't quite seemed to be able to recover from. The great blessing of the matter, though, is that because of the Spirit and because of the Divine Mind of the Godhead – our true and authentic nature – we are able to always able to begin making up for lost time. Scripture speaks very plainly about making up for times that have seemed lost. In fact, two passages of scripture come to mind. In Ephesians 5:15, the Apostle Paul speaks of "redeeming the time," and in Joel 2:25, the Lord declares through the prophet that He will repay us for the "lost years." In other words, it's possible to begin to live again and to enjoy the experiences of this life, like never before, no matter what you've gone through. I don't say that to be insensitive to your pain or to the heartbreak you've endured. I say that, rather, to encourage you and to say that regardless of what you encountered and regardless of the time you've wasted, you can begin to get it back today with a very simple, yet Divine shift of thinking.

It's time to move from the idea – the illusion – of separation and disconnectedness and begin to step into the full measure of inspiration. The voice of inspiration is continually calling out to you at all times. In literally each and every season, through each and every encounter and circumstance, the voice of the Spirit is encouraging you to begin to step out and to live again. It's amazing just how much life begins to flow in our favor the moment we finally begin to allow it. I choose to allow the universe to work in my favor. I refuse to allow it to work against me. I am a powerful spiritual being – the Divine Creator – and I will in no way allow the unexpected twists and turns to rob me of my valuable time and my valuable years.

If someone wishes to be in my life, I welcome them. If someone doesn't, then, with love, I wish them well and allow them to move on. Time is far too valuable to spend even a moment wasted on regret and worry and loneliness. The universe is far too big and far too expansive and, most of all, the Spirit is far too vast for me to ever feel disconnected and alone and without. I am always connected, at all times, to the resources and to the people I need within my life. Just as you are.

I encourage you to begin to recognize, today, that the artwork of your life, though it might appear to be quite messy at first glance, is truly a masterpiece being created. The Creator has placed His brush upon the canvas of your life with a very specific image in mind and has begun a "good work" in you which will be completed. With each and every stroke He begins to uncover a beauty already beheld within His mind's eye. With each stroke of His brush upon the canvas of your life, a masterpiece is beginning to come to life in new and exciting ways. Right now you may not be able to see the finished product, but hold on. Be patient. The colors are beginning to emerge from the canvas. A beautiful tapestry of experience is now being captured and brought to life.

The strokes seem very messy at first. The colors, though vibrant, seem so very scattered and out of place, at times. There is a method to what seems like madness, however, I assure you. Now, the Creator – the artist – lowers his brush to take a moment to admire his wonderful creation. He steps back and pauses with a sense of pleasure, looking onto the finished canvas. The Creator has given so much time and so much attention to the work that He can now call it "good." The Creator looks into the mirror. Now, for the first time, you see

yourself staring back. It had been a self-portrait
all along.

Living the Dream

All of creation is birthed within a dream. It would be impossible to speak to you of the subject of the Law of Creation without, also, speaking of the important aspect of the dream-state. As I've shared in many of my past teachings, the dream-state is by its very nature Divine and is, yet, another aspect of the Spirit world making itself known to us. I share much, much more of this in my book *The God Element Within Dreams* and in my *School of*

Visualization course, available through Identity Network. As we've discussed, you – well, the *real* you – are not the physical form which you currently inhabit. You are not the body you now live within. You are much more. You are the eternal – the *Endless*. You are the observer – the "watcher," if you will.

For every book now available upon the market dealing with the Law of Attraction, there are equally as many, if not more, dealing with the subject of dreams. Throughout humanity, we all, regardless of religion, creed, gender, or socioeconomic background, find ourselves upon an equal and balanced level playing field within the dream-state. We are all the same there. We are all equal. We are all, in the world of dreams, experiencing the eternal fabric of our connectedness. Dream interpretation is a pivotal aspect of the prophetic gifting. In fact, throughout the years, for every prophetic word I've delivered around the world, I've interpreted equally as many dreams. They can be so troubling, at times. They can give us hope. They can reveal to us even the most hidden and most covered aspects of our own natures. They always, though, show us something about the truth of the Spirit world.

There is a certain kind of transcendence about our dreams – an eternally ethereal quality. There is unity there. So much unity, in fact, that even the dead return to us, there, simply to reconnect and to remind us of the roles they played within our lives, when they, too, walked among the living, here, within the earthly plane. Our dreams, quite simply, remind us of our own, eternal spiritual nature by showing us that there is truly no time or distance or separation within the realm of the Spirit. Only days ago, as of the time of this writing, a dear friend reached out and asked that I give advice to him regarding what, to him, seemed to be a very troubling and disturbing dream he had just experienced. In it, he explained to me, he found himself seated within the congregation of a church, listening intently to the message being delivered. When suddenly – unexpectedly – and quite violently, a massive sword pierced through the ceiling and began to slice into the members of the congregation. "It was horrifying to see," he explained. "There was a very real sense of dread and danger," he shared.

Immediately, by the Spirit, I knew the meaning of the dream and offered my love and encouragement. "The sword represents a dividing between two worlds," I explained. "It represents a dividing between the world of flesh and the world of the Spirit." He said that my words resonated with him and that they served as confirmation. Quite often, prophetically, as I interpret dreams, I'm literally taken into the dream itself, and the Spirit allows me to witness the goings on and the happenings being described, even before the dreamer ever utters a word.

This, my friend, is the essence of the Spirit world – an eternal connectedness and the Oneness of who we truly are. Science has shown us, and continues to show us, that there is, in fact, a very real spiritual element within the dream state. While in the dream, our brains literally begin to operate differently than at other times. The question must be asked, then, does the brain change in order for us to dream, or does the dream change the human brain. The answer, quite simply, is both. Brainwaves, or *neural oscillation*, are the activity of the central nervous system. I share much more about this in my book *The Universe is at Your Command*. There is absolutely a scientifically proven correlation between the neural oscillation of the central nervous system and the neural pathways being formed during the experience. In other words, to put it much more simply, our dreams literally change us by awakening us.

Research shows that there are five, distinctly different types of brain waves – each leading to different levels of awareness and states of consciousness. As mystical, as it might seem to hear, my friend, yes, talk of consciousness is pivotal to talk of the Kingdom. One cannot truly speak of the awakened nature of the Kingdom of God, within, without speaking, also, of the different and deepening levels of human consciousness. In truth, it is utterly impossible to separate talk of the Kingdom of God from talk of human consciousness, because the realities of the Divine Mind – the inner, secret Kingdom spoken of by Jesus – is a realm deep *within*. When beginning to study brain activity, one finds that there are Beta waves, Alpha waves, Theta waves, Delta waves, and, lastly, Gamma waves. I want you to think of the brain, if you will, in terms of a transmitter within a radio receiver.

When speaking of brain activity, we are speaking in terms of frequency – literally, in terms of energy. Beta refers to the frequency of waking consciousness of normal, everyday life. The Alpha frequency is the frequency of deep relaxation. Theta waves refer to the state of light meditation or prayer and certain levels of sleep. Delta waves refer to the state of being in deep sleep. And Gamma waves are commonly referred to as the wave of insight and transcendence. Because brain activity creates literal, physical energy which can be measured by an electroencephalograph machine, or EEG, it can be confirmed, both, scientifically and medically, that the brain is radiating very specific frequencies at all times. Even now, as you read these words, your brain activity is continuously fluctuating between the wave of waking consciousness of alertness and the deeper waves of study and spirituality. Even the act of learning changes our brain waves. Science, in fact, proves that from a very early age we exist with a more heightened awareness and a heightened level of consciousness. Then, as we become older, we begin to forget our true nature and naturally become more anesthetized to the world of the Spirit.

Then, at the proper time, awakening comes, again. Thankfully. Delta wave activity is the most common activity found in infants and continues to be so until around the age of five years old. Meaning that children are, in fact, more prone to experience the spiritual realms than most adults who spent their days in normal activity. If you are the parent of a young child, never even for a moment think that the experiences your child recounts to you are simply aspects of having an over-active imagination. I am a firm believer that children do, in fact, see the angelic realm more than adults do. In fact, it isn't unusual for children to see and encounter angelic activity quote regularly! It's no wonder, really, that Jesus so often spoke of having childlike faith and simple belief. There's an openness, there – a doorway, of sorts. There is not yet the conditioning. The indoctrination. Children believe and therefore experience because they've never yet encountered religion saying to them, "It isn't real." Oh, to be childlike, again. We can become that again, though, you know? It's true. We can actually program, through careful practice each day, our minds to conform to the frequencies of the higher planes of existence.

Have you ever said a brief, repetitive prayer and felt nothing, yet, at other times, spent an extended period of time in deep prayer and meditation, only to feel a very real difference? Well, there's a very real scientific reason for this, my friend. As the brain waves are changed, the literal feeling is changed. I recently watched a very interesting study in which Pentecostal individuals were placed under careful study and their brain waves measured as they spoke in tongues.

Remarkably, the study found that as the participants spoke in tongues, the brain activity changed very quickly, indicating that there was a literal deepening of the state of consciousness. What if I were to tell you that the dream world is actually much more real than this temporal, physical world which we have been led to believe is reality? Would you find that shocking? If so, why? Scripture places very strong emphasis upon the correlation between the dream-state and spiritual activity. In fact, the Prophet Joel said that when the Spirit comes, there will always be very vivid dreams. In truth, the activity of the Spirit always brings with it three things: visions, dreams, and prophecy. The three are forever related. "And it shall come to pass afterward, that I will pour out my spirit upon all flesh; and your sons and your daughters shall prophesy, your old men shall dream dreams, your young men shall see visions. And also upon the servants and upon the handmaids in those days will I pour out my spirit." (Joel 2:28-29)

Upon the day of Pentecost, as the church was born and as the inner Kingdom awakened, the Apostle Peter, in Acts 2:17, confirmed that it was, indeed, the beginning of the last days, as the Spirit came and the age of prophecy was enacted. There was a new dispensation – there was an open Heaven. We find that in the Book of Acts, after the outpouring of the Spirit, angelic visitation became the norm. The miraculous became an ordinary part of everyday life. The supernatural became natural. Why? Because those who had finally, at the appointed and proper time become awakened, began to live within the dream. No longer was the dream-state confined to the shadows of the night but, now, the dreams had begun to come to life for all to see!

There was a merging, of sorts – a blending – between worlds. To the outside world – the physical world looking on – few could even tell where Heaven ended and the earth began. There was only one, single, movement of the Spirit permeating the earth realm, triggering the miraculous in each and every moment. The Law of Creation was now common place, daily. I share this with you to remind you that this is still your birthright. It's a normal aspect of the functioning of the Divine Mind. As wonderful as the occurrence were and as otherworldly as the supernatural world appeared to be, it was possible to go even deeper. My humble and sincere prayer for you, today, is that you would begin to move even deeper into the God element within your dreams.

Because your dreams are actually indicative of your eternal and spiritual connection with the Source. Scripture is replete with talk of visions and dreams and Heavenly encounters – moments at which the Spirit world literally merged with the land of the physical world. In Genesis 28, we find the dream depicting "Jacob's ladder." In Genesis 41, we find the importance of dream interpretation, as Joseph is given Divine ability to interpret dreams, after being given very detailed and otherworldly dreams of his own. Peter, while atop the roof of the home of Cornelius was given a vision which depicted the way in which the Kingdom would be awakened among the Gentiles.

Furthermore, on two other accounts, we find that certain individuals actually were taken into Heaven and shown the great mysteries of the Spirit. The Apostle Paul, in his own words, had an experience which was so otherworldly and so very transcendent that he didn't even know is he was actually in his own body! And, let us not forget that the entire Book of Revelation was written by the Apostle John while exiled upon the Isle of Patmos. His writing begins, "I was *in the spirit* on the Lord's day, and heard behind me a great voice, as of a trumpet." (Revelation 1:10) My friend, your dreams are not simply some escape from the real world, as many would have you believe. No, your dreams are the access point at which we are reminded of our own, true spiritual nature. The dream state is a very real state of existence and it is forever linked to the Law of Creation. I would be remiss if I did not share with you this truth in a much more practical way. For me, everything that I now have the privilege of experiencing in my own, personal life, for me, it began in dreams. The ministry, the outreach, the prophetic gifting, it all began within the dream-state. Even this book – these words you now read – began within the dream-state. It's there, in that eternal and ethereal realm of the spirit that I find my greatest inspiration.

You and I are always welcome in the realm of dreams, for it is, in truth, the realm of the Spirit in total and complete operation. It's the place at which we cease from striving and simply allow ourselves to *be*. While in the state of the dream, we are given direction, inspiration, encouragement, and edification. Businesses are birthed within dreams. Relationships are birthed within dreams. Riches and success are birthed within dreams. We are given warnings and Divine insight from the Divine mind of the Spirit while in the dream state. My friend, I want to encourage you, today, to begin to dream again.

Take time to become more aware of your dreams. In fact, begin taking time to ask Spirit to visit you and to help you to become more aware of your dreams. All that is required is a simple childlike faith in order to begin to experience the fullness of the supernatural world. By bringing the dream into the three-dimensional realm of physical space and time – here within the earth – we are literally making a decree to the universe that we are fully surrendered.

Energy of the Spirit

Knowing now that the Law of Creation goes hand-in-hand with the Law of Attraction and that the mind is literally creating a powerful and a very tangible energy which can be measured, both scientifically and medically speaking, I want to share with you an even greater understanding of the physics behind the spiritual realm – an even greater vantage point to see behind the scenes of the energy at work. In order to truly master the creation of your thoughts, we must remember that we are always radiating energy – both physically and spiritually. It cannot be said enough that thoughts are constantly creating a very real and tangible, recordable and measurable energy.

Did you know that your entire being – not only spiritually but also biologically and physiologically – was designed for the sole purpose of being able to harness energy? Yes, you read that correctly. Every single element of your physical, natural body was designed with the intention of energy in the Divine Mind of the Spirit. Suffice it to say, we were created for fellowship with the Spirit, both literally and figuratively speaking. We've discusses how even the brain is formed to harness the power of thought and how even out brainwaves – the neural oscillation – is continuously changing in order to take us into deeper realms of heightened or enlightened or "illuminated" consciousness, on order for us to have greater otherworldly experiences within the Spirit realm. Did you know that the rest of your body was designed for this same, specific function, as well? It's true.

Your entire body was designed by the Creator to initiate fellowship with the Spirit on all levels. Think of your body as a sort of transmitter or super conductor of the energies of the universe. So often I hear people talking about how they literally despise their human bodies. Well, first of all, it's possible to change what you don't like. But, also, it's important to recognize just how Divine your human body truly is. "I will praise thee; for I am fearfully and wonderfully made: marvelous are thy works; and that my soul knoweth right well." (Psalm 139:14) Were you aware that even the glands of the human body serve very specific functions related to Spirit communication? It's true and scientifically proven.

According to science, the human body is constantly and continuously emanating the energy of vibration, and these vibrations create an electromagnetic field around the body.

Every single function of the human body, from digestive function to the functions of the nervous system and circulatory system radiate energy and continuously make up a series of electromagnetic reactions, causing heat. Have trouble believing that? Look no further than the corpse of someone who has just taken their last breath within the physical world. Within mere minutes of the soul leaving the body at the point of death, when the systems of the physiological and biological body begin to shut down the temperature of the human body left behind begins to rapidly drop. The physical remains – the corpse – begins to feel cool to the touch. Why? Because the systems of the body internally are no longer functioning. My friend, this is a known fact.

In the living, human body, the electric and magnetic energy fields interact to form what is referred to as "The Bio-Energetic Field." This energetic field, commonly referred to as the "aura" by some, radiates outwardly from the human body approximately 4 to 5 feet at all times and consists of a variety of beautiful colors, most often unseen with the naked eye. Now, I know what you must be thinking. "Jeremy, that seems so 'new age.'" Well, my friend, call it whatever you wish to call it; however, it is a simple fact. We must become mature in our understanding of the body and of the mind and of the Spirit and grow into the greater knowledge of the inner Kingdom which Jesus spoke of. If it seems like a "new age" concept, then so be it. However, we, as a society, are perishing for lack of knowledge and wisdom because we have chosen to remain ignorant within the confined structures of our religious traditions, and I, for one, refuse to settle for a lack of knowledge.

Prophetically, I see these colors each and every day and have since first entering into the ministry. Often times, those who are sick and require physical healing emanate a darker, more muted and less vibrant energy, while those who are well and whole in all areas emanate and radiate a color much more like the colors of the rainbow. However, in truth, if you are reading this and breathing then you are emanating certain lights and colors. The very fact that you are alive and still within the physical body is proof positive that your bodily systems are still functioning – still creating energy and creating electromagnetic current. Research in the field of quantum physics has proven that literally everything in existence is energy. And one of the most basic and fundamental empirical laws of physics is that energy, by definition, can never be created or destroyed. It just simply *is*. It changes forms and continues to remain.

My friend, even science confirms the eternal nature of the soul and continues to, in its own way, remind humanity that there is, in fact, a very real afterlife. You are energy. You always have been. You always will be. Part of the reason that you will forever remain is the scientific truth that energy simply cannot be destroyed; it simply changes forms and continues to exist. Even the most simple movement of an atom will create a quantifiable electromagnetic field which can be measured. Just as an EEG is capable of measuring the activity of the brain, so, too, can something known as Kirlian photography measure and capture the energy radiating from the body. If the term "aura" is a term that you find yourself uncomfortable accepting, then, choose simply to refer to it as the "soul emanation." Think of it as the radiation of the soul – the soul's rainbow! Regardless, though of what you choose to call it and no matter how you choose to define the processes, it is ignorant to suggest that such things are not real, simply because the systems of religion have failed humanity for centuries by not providing it with the truth of creation. You may ask, "Jeremy, what does this energy have to do with the Law of Creation and the process of mastering my creation?" Well, the answer, quite simply, is, "Everything!" In case you have yet to notice, my friend, all of scripture is filled with accounts of the power of creation being entrusted to you and I.

You and I have been entrusted with the responsibility of creation, meaning that we are, each, responsible for the energy we've been given. It is our responsibility to maintain it well and to keep it in balance! The scriptures are filled, time and time again with the Spirit, in essence, saying, "This is *yours*, now what are *you* going to do with it?" The Spirit is continually asking us, "How are *you* going to use the energy of creation in your life?" I so often hear, time and time again, many sincere, well-intentioned people speaking of themselves as if they are nothing more than sinners saved by grace, good for very little else.

My friend, not only is that mindset not scriptural at all, the grace which awakened us is also the same grace that empowers us! If you are choosing to not awaken to your own creative power and utilizing the power of your mind to create a better and more fulfilling life for yourself, then you are literally allowing your religion to make the Word of the God void. Jesus, himself, said that it was religious tradition which makes the Word powerless. "Making the word of God of none effect through your tradition, which ye have delivered: and many such like things do ye." (Mark 7:13) My friend,

I do not say this to condemn or to judge but, rather to encourage you and to edify you and to inspire you. I say this with all love and grace: Your religion is killing you and it is weakening your energy and dulling the colors of your rainbow. My prayer for you is that you would begin to recognize just how damaging the tradition of religion is to the power of God. Scripture tells us that in select settings even Jesus, himself, could do no mighty works because of unbelief and religious tradition. As we've discussed, there is a correlation – a very real link – between the beliefs and thoughts we possess and the energy we create with our thoughts and the energy the body radiates. It's all connected. It's all interwoven. When one energy system is out of balance then all other systems of the energy field are out of balance, also.

My friend, I would encourage you to begin to stop allowing the man-made systems of religion and tradition to interfere with the systems of the Spirit working and flowing through you. You will either obey man, or you will obey God. As Peter said in Acts 5:29, "We ought to obey God rather than men." If you find yourself thinking, "Jeremy, I can't believe this," well, that's the problem. It's unbelief that produces the mindset of disconnectedness and separation – the antithesis of Oneness. Do the scriptures not teach us that literally everything rises and falls upon our belief or unbelief?

Today, I want to encourage you to begin to not only see the energy of the Spirit as a powerful force of creation, working in conjunction at all times with your thoughts, but I want you to also see that your very own body plays a major role in conducting this energy. Your entire body is a giant conductor of the creative power of the universe, and your thoughts are the fuel that raises the level of force. I want to share with you a secret that I learned years ago that has not only helped me in my own life and ministry but also in business and in my friendships and in my relationships:

You are responsible for guarding your own energy. Scripture speaks of guarding the heart. What it means, in truth, is that we must learn to guard our minds. "Keep thy heart with all diligence; for out of it are the issues of life." (Proverbs 4:23) In other words, all life and everything related to life – literally everything that we encounter on a daily basis – stems from the thoughts and from the energy field we're radiating. It's up to us to guard it. Though we can and should and must love everyone, there are some people who simply should not be allowed access into our energy fields. Some people have no business being allowed access into our lives. Begin to think more highly of yourself. See yourself as having more value. You truly do.

There are some individuals who simply are not in covenant with us, and it's important that we begin to correctly discern the energies – the true intentions – of others and begin to guard our energies more. I have a friend who, like me, is very sensitive to energy – very empathic, just as I am. He describes his experiences with energy in this way: "It's like a black suit. You need one. But if you're gonna have one, you also need a lint roller, because it'll pick up everything." It's true, though. All throughout the day, your energy is like Velcro, not only attaching to the things we want but also picking up every piece of lint and fuzz imaginable. This is how energy fields work! Don't believe that? Just think of how often you've entered a room filled with people and suddenly gotten a bad "vibe" or felt uncomfortable. We casually dismiss this feeling as nothing more than nervousness. It's the Spirit speaking. Or, perhaps even more common, how often have you had a conversation with someone, only to feel so drained and so weighed down after walking away? It's because you've literally picked up their energy! Their energy has literally clung to you. We're all always working with electromagnetic energy at all points throughout the day.

This is why visualization, prayer, and meditation are absolutely vital. Meditation is like the "lint roller" of the Spirit. Each and every day, we must take time to not only discern our own energy fields but also learn to immediately recognize, "This feeling isn't mine. It doesn't belong to me," and remove the extra added weight. Oh, my friend, how I pray you would grab hold of this powerful truth. There are energies that have weighed you down that were never even your burden to carry. The relationship that ended, let it go and move on. The person that you spent years giving love and grace to, who, in turn, continues to give you nothing but disrespect and manipulation, let them go and begin to guard your heart in a better way. You deserve better. So often I see so many powerful people beginning to lose their own sense of power and become a punching bag

171

or a door mat for other people. The people that we expect to give us love and honor or so very often the people who give the most weight to carry. Let it go! This life is too short, and time is far too valuable and the energies of creation are far too precious to continue carrying dead weight. As scripture teaches, lay aside every "weight." Sometimes, this means people. The truth of the "demonic" is not simply that there are malevolent entities trying to attack you in the spiritual realm.

No, the truth of the matter is that so very often there are forces, here and now, in the form of people, places, and situations, that are dead set and Hell-bent on attaching to your energy field. Like vampires they begin to drain us of our life source. Today, begin to take stock of your own energy field. Guard it. Protect it. Most importantly and above all, learn to discern it correctly. Begin to gain a heightened sensitivity in the Spirit to see the energies and the true intentions of others. I cannot stress enough that you and you, alone, are responsible for your own energy. The universe has already entrusted you with all the power of the Godhead. Stop expecting God to change what you, yourself, are not willing to change. I promise you, He will not.

Sound and Color

The canvas of creation is painted by a brush that has been dipped onto the palette of all the colors of existence. To recognize this, one need only to see the outside world for a moment. From the beauty of trees and the sound of flowing streams to the sound of your favorite band and the touch of the hand of your mate, life is filled with many diverse and interesting beautiful colors. These colors emanate, as we've discussed, though, not only

from the outside world but, too – most of all –
from a very real inside world. All color and
sound, as we've discussed, radiates from within,
at the level of the thought. Not only does
creation, itself, radiate with the resonance and
frequency of the breath of the Divine Mind but,
too, we, ourselves, also are in a constant state of
vibration.

With each movement within the central nervous
system – with neural oscillation – to the very
words we speak, the whole earth is vibrating
and moving. It's shaking. Sound and color are
intrinsically interwoven into creation and, as
powerful observers – we are always in a
position to enact upon it with our own desires,

based entirely upon our thoughts. Sound and color are connected. For this reason, the tones that we emit on a daily basis have great significance. It's impossible to think a thought or to speak a word without, also, changing the energy of existence. Not only do our thoughts matter and our words matter but, so, too, does the way in which we speak matter.

In my prophetic ministry, I so often counsel many who are involved in different areas of business – particularly heads of business and CEOs of companies. What I tell leaders of business who are entering into negotiations or preparing for important meetings is, "It's not just *what* you say, it's *how* you say it that matters." Tones matter. "A *soft* answer turneth away wrath: but grievous words stir up anger." (Proverbs 15:1) Sound matters. Inflection matters. Vocal resonance matters. How often have our true intentions so often been lost in translation simply because of *how* we said *what* we said? It happens day in and day out. Arguments begin because of tone. Things fall apart and confusion arises because, simply, the way in which we speak so often isn't in alignment with our true intentions or thoughts. With a slight imbalance, the entire world can rise and fall. Wars have begun over far, far less. History, itself, shows us this truth.

I was speaking to a young woman once who had just met a young man. They were preparing to go to dinner together for the very first time. "I can't wait to see you this evening," she said in a text. He replied, quite simply, "Me too." Now, as much as he truly did anticipate the evening out, his lackluster and seemingly nonchalant response caused quite a stir. "He just didn't seem very interested," she explained to me. Fortunately the confusion ended after the evening; however, I share this with you to simply say that tones and inflections matter. In a world of text, confusion arises when communication isn't fully expressed. We have to be more careful, now, more than ever before, to convey our true intentions correctly. Hence, again, personal responsibility.

I'm a student of, both, history and science. When I was completing my doctoral thesis for my doctorate in Divinity, I came to find few things more beautiful than the sound of the Aramaic language. It was the language of Jesus. As shocking as it may be to the religious mindset, especially here in westernized culture, contrary to popular belief, Jesus did not speak English. Furthermore, the Bible, as we now know it, wasn't written in English, originally. Shocking, I know. It wasn't even written in the King's English. That wouldn't come until centuries later, in 1611. As most of the popular films depicting the life of Jesus portray, Jesus didn't even speak with as British accent. Again, shocking, I know.

Theologically speaking, the scriptures that we have come to know and love and use as the foundation of our lives have gone through many, many changes throughout the centuries, now coming to us in the form that we're most familiar with. To prove this fact, one needs only to go to the local Christian bookstore and visit the Bible section. There are so, so many to choose from, now! If words truly matter, as I know they do, then this should be concerning to us. I digress, though. Suffice it to say that words matter. Theologically speaking, the scriptures were first passed down orally, after the events transpired. Then, written records were transcribed and compiled. Time passed. The Gospel continued to be spread. Religion arose. Man-made systems and institutions of religion sought to manipulate and control.

For the longest time, in cultures and society's in which the masses were illiterate, most depended upon the priest or preacher to share with them the words of the scriptures. There was very little personal knowledge of the scriptures, as we now have the ability to access, in the modern age we now find ourselves in. There was, first, the compilation into the Greek language. Then, into Latin. Centuries later, arriving into the court of King James. Throughout the centuries, though, languages changed. Meanings of words changed. Not to patronize, but I hope you do know that the disciples didn't carry Bibles. I mean, you do know that, right? They were familiar with the Law of Moses, and they were familiar with the prophets and the history of Israel. In fact, it was the Law of Moses that serves as the basis of the Judaism of the ancient world which produced the Pharisees Jesus walked among. Suffice it to say, the Word of God came throughout centuries, in very interesting ways.

The Spirit moved upon men and inspired them. However, the scriptures, as we now know them, came, originally, from the Aramaic language. The Aramaic alphabet was adopted by other languages and is the ancestral language to the Syriac and Arabic language. It is also ancestral to the Hebrew language. So, to say, simply, that the Old Testament was written in Hebrew and the New Testament was written in Greek is a misnomer. It's true, yes; however, to say that doesn't do justice to the history of the language. It all began with a dialect of Aramaic.

Texts were written, originally, in Biblical Aramaic, sometimes referred to as "Classical Hebrew." Classical Hebrew is an archaic form of Hebrew, synonymous with the alphabet of original Aramaic. So, that being said, Aramaic and Hebrew are from the same family. Having a proper understanding of linguistics helps us to do justice to the history of the scriptures. Now, that being said – now that we've established a proper working understanding of the language of the Bible – what does that truly mean for us? For you and I? Understanding that the tones of our words matter, there is absolutely nothing like the tone and the sound of the Aramaic language. It's unique. It's beautiful. I've studied it for decades.

People often ask, "Jeremy, how do you have such insight into the scriptures?" Well, it's by the Spirit, yes, but it's also by study. Having now within the pages of this book established the foundation of the truth of energy, color, and sound, allow me to share with you what this truly means for you and I, in this modern time. Allow me to share with you the deeper, hidden mysteries of this truth of the Law of Creation and how it is entirely dependent upon color and sound and vibration. "Your words are your worship." Yes, you read that correctly.

You are always worshipping and creating an image to worship, within your mind. So often, because of religious tradition, we are taught to believe that worship is strictly relegated to a church service, when the music minister and the choir or the praise team takes the stage. Though that is a form of worship, you are worshipping right now. We are always, with our thoughts and with our words, worshipping *something*. With every word, you are worshipping because with every sound, you are emitting a call into the universe around you to create. Stay with me now. Every word and every tone is a vibrational sound and color which is painting the world you now find yourself in. Every single word. Every single tone. It's creating a color and a resonance and frequency which is a command.

When I wrote my best-selling book *The Universe is at Your Command*, I did so with this truth at the heart of the matter. The energy you are radiating is the command you are giving to the universe. Your tone is your worship. Have you ever noticed, my friend, in your study of the scriptures, that the cloud by day and the pillar of fire by night – the visible and manifest presence of the Lord which led the children of Israel out of Egypt – appeared to lead them only after they had stepped out of their captivity?

I mean, as the people of God, had He not always been with them, as He had promised Abraham? Yet, we find that only at a very specific time, did the presence of God visibly manifest for all to see, only *after* they had stepped out from the mindset of Egypt. My friend, so often the reason you do not see the fruit of the land which you wish to see is because you unknowingly still have so much of Egypt remaining in your thinking. In Exodus chapter 12, we find that there was a time of purging and cleansing before the Exodus even occurred. For weeks prior to the Exodus, the children of Israel were instructed to prepare themselves to move forward. In other words, they needed to get their minds right. They needed to get their thoughts right.

For days and even weeks prior to the migration from Egypt the people were instructed to speak to their families of the promises of God. Study the scriptures. It was only after they had prepared their minds and spoke to one another of the promises of God that the Exodus was finally allowed to happen. And when it did, the very place that had served as a place of captivity instantly became a place of blessing, as even the Egyptians gave away their riches to the children of Israel. Talk about the Law of Attraction at work! Furthermore, though, there were sounds of rejoicing. There were continuous stories being told of the power of the Spirit.

We often erroneously teach that the visible presence of God manifested only once the tabernacle was completed. Not so. It manifested as a cloud and as a pillar of fire the instant the children of Israel emitted a tone and a sound that created a vibration that changed their poverty mindset to a mindset of prosperity and riches! In other words, they began to attract the promises of God within their own lives! You see, there was a sound, and there was color. There was a visible sight being radiated for all to see. The same with the tabernacle of David and the temple of Solomon. There was a visible glory because there were continuous tones and sounds being offered up.

Even in Acts 2, we find that there is a correlation between sound and color. There were flames of fire and the uttering of sound. Why do I share this with you? Because there is a very real correlation between what you're seeing and what you're saying. The two are dynamically linked! Stop talking like you're still in Egypt as a slave! You aren't merely some wretched sinner saved by grace; the grace has made you not only a king but also the Creator!

I share this with you because each and every day, whether you realize it consciously or not, you are emitting tones and sounds and colors that are destroying your life by keeping you within a prison of an old mindset. "I don't believe it." Why is he rich while I have to struggle?" "Why did she just buy a new car?" "I can't believe they're really that happy together." "I guess God doesn't want me to have nice things." "Money is the root of all evil." My friend, if these are the tones and the sounds of your creation, you will die in poverty.

If these are the sounds you're sending as your command to the universe you will continue to work the job that you hate that's draining your life. You'll never attract the mate you desire and will die alone. You will always live paycheck to paycheck, barely getting by and struggling to make ends meet. I share this with you, with all love and grace, to say that you are literally killing yourself with the sound you are emitting into the universe around you. I refuse to live in lack. I won't do it. I deserve to be blessed. I deserve to be wealthy, and I know it. So do you. And if you hear me speak of wealth and automatically think of money, then you're in an ignorant mentality and are immature. Wealth means far, far more than just money and material things. Wealth is a mindset of abundance. More peace. More joy. More power of the Spirit. With that, though, will come more money! Hear me now, my friend. When you begin to surrender to the mind of the Spirit, you will then, in turn, bring into your life all that the Spirit possesses, which is all things. Yes, there will be more money.

My friend, did you know that the world requires wealth? Rich people are needed in the world. If you don't believe that and if you have trouble wrapping your mind around that then perhaps you should quit your job and stop receiving a paycheck. A wealthy, rich man or woman is responsible for giving it to you. You see, there is, both a place and a need for more abundance in this physical world.

Why not allow yourself to begin to view yourself as one who deserves to be the recipient of the blessings of the universe. By setting the proper tone and the proper sound, you are placing yourself into the proper vibrational frequency to attract and to manifest what it is you truly want and desire. Do you truly wish to see change in your life? Then, more than changing your thoughts and more than changing your words and more than changing your actions, change your tone.

Soul Secrets

There was an instant – that point of incarnation – at which the ageless and eternal spirit became infused with the soul. In order to have a more proper understanding of our true identity and out own creative power, as it relates to the eternal Law of Creation, we must begin to recognize that there is a stark contract which exists between the spirit and the soul. You, even now, are an eternal spirit. A powerful thinking spirit, capable of manifesting all that your heart desires and intends and possessing the knowledge of how to enact the will of the Divine Mind from whence you've come. The soul, however, is relatively new to you in this incarnation. That element of the Self is still learning – still integrating and still learning to adapt. In the very beginning, you were known by the Creator, as you were at home in complete union with the Divine Mind. He knew us. As we find in the book of Jeremiah, as the Spirit speaks to through the prophet, he reminds us of our true identity. "Before I formed thee in the belly I knew thee.; and before thou camest out of the womb I sanctified thee, and I ordained thee a prophet unto the nations." (Jeremiah 1:5) The word for "knew" in the original language of the scripture is the term "YADA," which means to know intimately. Think of that beautiful truth. Again, we find the great depiction of Oneness contained within the scriptures. We see, again, that we not only existed as one with the Creator, within the Divine mind of the Spirit, but that we were also so at one with Him that there was complete and total intimacy.

There was no separation of distinction of identity even in the very beginning. This Divine union, though, is speaking only of the realm of the spirit. You see, we were at one with God and known by God from the perspective of the Spirit. We existed within Him as powerful, thinking spirits. However, when the moment of incarnation came – the point at which we, as powerful spirits, came into the world of the flesh – we came in contact with the realm of the soul. In order for us to have a proper working knowledge and understanding of the Law of Creation as it relates to the power of our own creative thoughts, it is important that we recognize the very real and important difference between the realm of the spirit and the realm of the soul.

Here, within this world of physicality and matter, we have been thrust into experiences which trigger our soul. Just as the nature of the Godhead is comprised of three components – the Father, the Son, and the Holy Ghost – so, too, are we made up of three aspects, in His eternal image. We have a spirit, a soul, and a body. The soul, itself, possesses three elements of existence: the mind, the will, and the emotions. Scripture gives us a glimpse into the elements of the soul and confirms to us that there are, indeed, three elements, each possessing specific function. Psalm 139:14 refers to the knowledge of the mind, as it relates to the soul. "My soul *knows* it well." Lamentations 3:20 refers to the memory of the soul: "My soul remembers them well."

This shows us that the soul is directly correlated with the mind and with thinking. The second aspect of the soul is the will. We find accounts within scripture of the soul being tied to the will and to choices made. Job 7:15 says, "My soul would *choose*," and in Job 6:7, we find a passage which says, "My soul refuses." In other words, concerning the aspect of the soul regarding choice, scripture makes it clear that the will is a part of the soul. Lastly, Song of Songs 1:7 and Psalm 42:1 reminds us that love is an aspect of the soul. Emotion is tied directly to the soul.

The Greek term for soul is "psyche," while the term for spirit is "pneuma," showing us, yet again, that there is a very real distinction between the spirit and the soul. The moment a baby is brought forth into the world, he or she is given a taste of the realm of the soul. At the point of incarnation, the powerful and eternal spirit is given the ability to think, to decide and to make choices, and to feel emotion. While at one with the Divine Mind of the Spirit, there was no need for such things. There was no need to cry, and there was no need for food. While in the realm of the Spirit, there was simply existence and balance.

Here, though, a new dimension brings with it new needs and new ways of expression. As the baby opens its human eyes for the first time to see the blinding light of the delivery room and the faces of the doctors, the soul realm become real in a very shocking way. Then, hunger sets in – a need to be fed. So begins the process of life within the realm of the soul. The realm of the soul is a realm of constant conditioning and learning and programming. Paradigms are continually formed within the mind, as decisions are made and as experiences are gained. The ability to reason and to think – elements of the soul – cause the being to begin to reinforce certain ideas and to lean certain concepts.

How different the soul realm is from the realm of the spirit. The realm of the soul can quite often feel like a a realm of separation. Though, it isn't, in reality, it can so often seem this way. So, so many factors contribute to the soul experience – to the many aspects of programming and conditioning that are to be experienced here within this natural world. Let us make it more practical, shall we? The baby born into the life of luxury will, because of the environment, have vastly different experiences from the baby born to the single mother, often struggling to provide. Though the ability to feel is completely identical, the experiences which will come to reinforce belief and thought and opinion are drastically different.

You see, it is for this reason that, though we are all the same in the spiritual essence, we are each unique in our thoughts and experiences. Because our conditioning is unique, so, too, are our emotions and out feelings. It is important to understand this truth as we speak of the power of the mind and of the eternal Law of Creation. Partly because it is important that we come to recognize just how identical we truly are in the spiritual sense, but also because it helps us to recognize our own, creative power of thought.

You, my friend, are now the product of a journey of your very own soul in this dimension of space and time. Your life, as you now see it and experience it, is the direct result of the way in which you have processed your own experiences and surroundings. Your very lifestyle is a direct result of how you have processed the world around you. With each and every thought we have, we are literally establishing a kingdom and a domain around us. Literally, right now in this moment, you are the product of the way in which you have interpreted the world around you. You, just as I, are the product of your thoughts. We have been given the ability to rationalize and to reason – to make decisions and to learn.

Truly, we are the creators of our life experiences, in that we, ourselves, are given the Divine power and ability to reason and to learn and to, either, adapt or change our environment. A lifestyle is a decision. So often, the most dangerous words our minds can ever utter are, "This is just the way it is." So often, we settle.

We tell ourselves that the environment around us is our permanent location. We determine, within our own thoughts, that it's far more easy to stay than to recreate and to advance. Comfort sets in. We find ourselves in a feeling of isolation and helplessness. A feeling of helplessness can quite often lead to a feeling of hopelessness. In fact, the two are quite synonymous.

The truth of the mater, though, my friend, is that you are not helpless and you most certainly aren't hopeless. It is the mind – the thought – which is leading you and has done so the entire time. Hear me, my friend, when I say with all love and with all grace that you are not the product of your environment or circumstances. You are the product of what you have chosen to think and believe about your environment and circumstances. Therein lies the very real truth of why you now find yourself living the life you now awaken to each and every day. Oh, please hear me when I say that you are not helpless. Never once have you been without the ability to change and to make choices which would lead to alternative outcomes and different roads.

Far too often we settle for the road most frequently traveled – settling for the norm – rather than choosing to take the road less traveled and awaken to our own creative power within the earth. When I birthed Identity Network, all those years ago, I had no way of knowing the vast and tremendous success which was awaiting me just on the other side of the doorway. I simply knew that I had a desire to awaken others the way the Spirit had awakened me. I realized, very early on, that it is , in fact, the mind, the will, and the emotions which either create our life experiences. In other words, it's what we *think* about life that determines the outcome of life.

Your experiences, today, will not define you. Yes, they are contributing factors which must continually be assessed and analyzed and reasoned; however, it is truly what you think about the experiences that will determine the way forward. Please hear me when I say to you that you are not where you are today by accident. You are now in the life you find yourself by Divine design and by your own creation. This is the grand truth behind the Law of Creation and the Law of Attraction. That we, all, have the power to change and to create anew and afresh and to always and forever become much, much more awakened to the greater truths of the mind. When awakening comes, we are given a mirror by which to view our lives. We, then, are given a very real choice.

The burden of change begins with accepting the burden of personal responsibility.

Today, as always, the Divine Mind of the Spirit is asking that you begin to take stock in the experiences of your life. Begin to see how you, just as at all other times, are the greatest contributing factor to your own life. No one else will change your life for you – no, not even God. Why would He? He has already given you and I all that we need in order to create. Just as the Lord spoke through the prophet Jeremiah, reminding him of his true identity, I wish to remind you, today, that you have never been without your true and authentic nature – that of the Creator.

You see, although the soul and the spirit are very different, with each possessing very different attributes and traits, never once have you been separated from your true spiritual nature. You are the Creator, Himself, having an earthly experience. What an amazing and beautiful truth, if you think about it. The burden of personal responsibility is your cross to bear. The cross is yours alone, just as I have my own cross to bear. You see, there in is the truth of the creation's eternal power throughout the cosmos. You and I, both, possess the same power.

Today, I want to not only encourage you to begin to see the immense and vast power which you have – which you've always had – but, even more so, I want to invite you to come along on an exciting journey of creation. I want you to join me and many, many others in being able to see the power of the universe at your disposal. This power is not foreign to you, though it may so often feel that way, at first. You're very familiar with the power of which I speak. This power, which formed the worlds, is the power of your very own being. Although you are now, in this life, experiencing a very real and different experience of the soulish realm, you are still the same, eternal, thinking spirit you've always been. Incarnation into the physical world did not change that. In fact, nothing did. The only different between *here* and *there*, is that *here*, we've convinced ourselves that *there* is separate and somehow apart from us. My friend, that's simply not the case. While we're here, within the world of flesh, with its many unique experiences and the joys and the pains which accompany them, we are not separate from each other and we are not separate from the Divine Mind of Spirit – the Source of all things. No. In fact, now, more than ever before, you and I are being asked to simply remember who we truly are. If you could begin to see each experience of each and every moment as but a teacher to you, rather than an enemy attempting to keep you imprisoned, I swear to you that you will finally realize the doors to the prison cell had been open all along.

Merging

Knowing, now, that there is, in fact, a very real and very important difference which exists between the realm of the spirit and the realm of the soul, I want to write to you concerning the process of integration. In other words, the great and necessary balance of it all. As we now know, scripture is replete with beautiful imagery and powerful, prophetic words which speak to us of our eternal Oneness with the Godhead and of our eternal Oneness with each other. There is, truly, no time or distance in the realm of the Spirit. There is no disconnectedness and no fragmentation. There is no dichotomy or duality. Here, though, in this earthly world of matter within the realm of physicality, I know it doesn't seem that way. In fact, I know that here, it can so often feel like quite the opposite. My friend, you and I were never designed to operate based solely upon our temporary feelings, however. You and I were designed to operate and to live and to experience with the knowing of the Divine Mind. Religion, with its many unnecessary rule and regulations and, above all, its many elementary fear-based concepts, propagates a childish understanding of God and of all creation. It attempts to place into the hands of the Creator that power that He has already given us. As a result, we learn to see, both, God and ourselves as being somewhat bipolar.

We come to believe, because of this false sense of dualism that God is love, yet he wishes to judge all the earth and to cast into "Hell" all who simply do not accept His love – it's so unlike the Divine nature. Yet, we are told and commanded, even, that we are to love and to never judge. I often find it rather humorous that religion attempts to paint a God to us who commands us to do the very opposite of what it says He's like. I digress, though. Let's just say, for the purposes of this book, that religion has not only caused more division and separation and chaos than one could even document within the pages of a book but it has, also, continued to fuel the idea of separation and disconnectedness with its many false and fear-based teachings of judgement.

My friend, God is not bipolar. God is not schizophrenic. He does not have multiple personality disorder. Never once has He ever had a nervous breakdown. He does not operate through psychosis. Yet, as religion would have us believe, He's very unstable. Both, a God of love and a God of vengeance. I would humbly, respectfully, and lovingly encourage to truly begin to the know the truth of God for your own life. Stop relying upon others to attempt to paint for you an image of the Creator that, in truth, looks absolutely nothing like the Creator. I invite you to experience the Spirit for your own life. It has been said that experience is, in fact, the very best teacher. I know that to be true. Scripture encourages us to "taste" and "see" that the Lord is good! In other words, you and I are continuously being invited to experience! What is it, though, about the life here within the physical plane of existence which so often causes us to feel so very disconnected and isolated and alone? Why is it that while we're here, we so often experience such a fragmentation of consciousness? Why is it that, while here, we begin to feel so very lost? I would submit to you that it's perception. Furthermore, it's perception based upon a false premise and a false narrative of duality.

I cannot stress to you enough that you are one with the Godhead and with the Divine Mind of the Spirit. The idea of separation is illusionary. For this reason, not only is it paramount that we possess a very real spiritual sensitivity, but it is essential that we gain a great understanding and working knowledge of who we truly are. You and I, existing in perfect harmony within God, have, seemingly, been thrust into a world of such apparent contradiction and confusion. As a result, there seems to be a chaos that abounds.

However, what if I were to respectfully submit to you that the apparent chaos is existing simply because we've forgotten? That we've forgotten where we've come from and that we've forgotten where we're going. Most of all that we've forgotten how truly interconnected we are, while we're here. It is so important that we begin to merge more into the aspects of the Divine Mind of the Spirit of God. The Spirit of God *is* the Spirit of truth. It is the Spirit which reminds us of our true identity and also of our own creative power. It is truly impossible to begin to master the creative power of our thoughts until we begin to integrate much more fully, in our understanding, into the mind of the Spirit.

As the Apostle Paul admonished, "Let *this* mind be in you." Oh, my friend, there is so very much to be said about *this* mind – the mind of the Spirit. It was *this* mind which formed the worlds throughout the cosmos and hurled onto the canvas of the cosmos thee stars and the many, many recesses of the galaxy, just as a painter paints upon the canvas. You and I witnessed it as it happened. You and I were there. We were there within Him. We were *in* Him. Because of the truth of Jesus, we are *in* Him now. Never once were we ever separated from Him. We simply allowed our understanding to be darkened here within the realm of the soul. There, again, the question must be asked: "What is it about *this* world which causes us to feel so lost?"

The Apostle Paul, in his epistles, uses beautiful and revelatory imagery to paint to us a picture of our unique state of being. He compares our knowledge, here, to being only finite and only in-part. That is, until awakening comes. "For now we see through a glass, darkly; but *then* face to face: *now* I know in part; but *then* shall I know even as also I am known." (1 Corinthians 13:12) What does this mean? Truly? This passage of scripture has very little to do with some future time, as we have been led to believe and much, much more to do with responsibility upon our part, in the here and now.

The Kingdom of Heaven has never once been about the *there* and *then*. It has always been, rather, about the *here* and the *now*. Paul, in his epistle to the church as Ephesus, also admonishes, "The eyes of your *understanding* being *enlightened*; that ye may *know* what is the hope of his calling, and what the riches of the glory of his inheritance in the saints." (Ephesians 1:18) Oh, how very beautiful. Oh, how transcendent. The Apostle Paul spoke plainly of a point – a moment – at which understanding would come. He was referring to the awakening of the mind. In other words, to put it much more plainly, my friend, Paul was speaking, rather directly, about the reality that we can *know*, now, the full measure of the truth.

In both epistles to the church at Thessaloniki, Paul speaks continuously about the "Day of the Lord." He even corrects himself. He first writes and says that it has come, only to then write, again, and say that it had not come. You see, throughout the writings of Paul we find that he, himself, was even in the process of coming into greater knowledge. He was continuing to move into greater understanding and more insight, just as you and I are. He was no different.

We so often think of the apostles, the prophets, the great teachers of the Spirit as somehow being more than human. However, the truth of the matter is that, like you and I, they were being continuously ushered into greater depths of revelatory knowledge, day by day. What I believed ten years ago, I no longer believe today. You could say the same, if you were honest with yourself. No, it isn't that I changed my mind, necessarily. I simply came into greater truth, just as we all do. Scenery is continuously changing upon the journey of the Spirit. We are ushered into greater glories and far greater truths. We move from "glory" to "glory." A better way to say it is that we are moving from "understanding" to "understanding."

You see, in order to master the power of the thought form and to have a proper understanding of the truth of the Law of creation, we must continually merge more deeply into the mind of the Spirit. Many people claim to hate sushi. And *then* they try it. I use this analogy to say that it is our experiences here which are the contributing factors of our thoughts; yet, so often we never want to move into new experiences. It's the same, spiritually speaking. For far too long, we've chosen to settle for the current surrounding – the current belief – the entire time saying, "This is all there is." Well, my friend, not only is this not all there truly is, the reality is that it isn't even a fraction of what truly is. There is more!

By learning to merge into the mind of the Spirit, we are, in essence, bringing our thoughts back into Divine alignment and thereby recognizing the truth of who we've always been. Oh, how I pray that you will receive this powerful, revelatory truth! The moment that you begin to see your thoughts through the filter of the Divine Mind, never again will you question your worth and never again will you question your life. You will, then, recognize that you are not the captive prisoner of your surroundings. No. In fact, it is quite the contrary. Your thoughts are subject to you. The entire world around you is.

In writing this book, as a follow-up to my book *The Universe is at Your Command: Vibrating the Creative Side of God*, I do so with the intention of bringing you into the even deeper knowledge of the Spirit. There are old paradigms that must be brought down – old, vain imaginations and false humilities that must be put to death – in order for you to merge more deeply into the Divine Mind of the Spirit. You see, there are always, at all times, continuous inner processes occurring in which you and I are being asked by the universe, "Is this the life you truly want?" However, for far too long, most have simply assumed that we, as humans, have absolutely no say in the matter.

Like the many primitive and archaic doctrines of religion, by having this belief, they find themselves being tossed about upon the wind. However, when awakening comes – when enlightenment comes – everything changes. A new paradigm is enacted and, with it, a new understanding. With awakening comes a new ability to see. We, then, are given the ability to move from a place of childlike believing to a place of illuminated knowing. There is a difference between the two. In our encounters with the Spirit, we are to be as little children, always possessing an openness.

However, in our understanding of spiritual truth, we must be mature, having come into the full measure of the knowledge of God.

Today, you are being given a choice. Will you settle for the current mindset of limitation, or will you, rather, step into the greater truth of the Spirit, into deeper understanding? The choice has always been yours, my friend. People often find it quite shocking when they hear me say to them that the Lord will do nothing else. I don't say that to be shocking or to be offensive; however, I know this to be the truth. Jesus, himself, said, "It is finished!" You see, so very often, because of the mindset of the religion, which is contrary at all times to the mind of the Spirit, we so often have this image of God seated upon a throne, continuously making decisions regarding our life. My friend, that isn't even scriptural! Study the scriptures! "Surely the Lord GOD will do nothing, but he revealeth his secret unto his servants the prophets." (Amos 3:7)

Now, in this world of ours, we possess the power which He has given us – the revelation of the truth of the Spirit. The moment you begin to stop waiting on the universe to give you the life you truly desire and begin to, instead, create the life you dream of by accessing your own, creative power, never again will you ever settle for the lifeless, cold, dead man-made religions of this earth. My friend, I pray that you get a revelation for your own life. Begin to prophesy to your own life through your own thoughts and begin to declare that your world is subject to you!

Oh, where would we be, were in not for the power of the Spirit within our lives? Truly lost. It is the Spirit who not only gives life but, as we now know, gives us direction. As I have seen for decades, the prophetic voice is integral to the power of manifestation within the life of an individual. There must be an agreement. An agreement not only with the voice of the Spirit but, too, an agreement within our own selves. My friend, we simply cannot afford to be double minded and tosses about by every wind of religious doctrine. There is far, far too much at stake.

I say this to offer to you a word of encouragement, in hopes of inspiring you to recognize that you are, even now, in a position to begin to reshape your life with the power of the thought form. You are even now – more so now, in fact, that you have been awakened – in a position to begin to reshape your life to conform to the image you have always dreamed of and imagined. The journey of the soul, in this realm, is a journey of limitless potential and imagination. As I have shared with you, you are, indeed, responsible for the creation of your life. You, just as I, have been infused with the power of creation in order to enact, within the earth realm, al that you desire. You have been Divine called to create at will, for your own, good pleasure.

Today, I encourage you with all love and grace to begin to recognize just who you truly are. The power of prophecy has always and forever will be, above all, a voice of inspiration. Throughout the years, I have been so very humbled and privileged to witness, firsthand, the power of the prophetic operating in the lives of individuals, just like you. Like you, they, too, longed for a better life. We're all the same, really, in that, at the most core and basic element, we all possess the dreams and the desires of fulfillment. We all desire a much more abundant life. It's really no wonder that Jesus spoke of fulfillment and of the inner Kingdom in terms of a more fulfilling life.

I've witnessed, firsthand, in my travels throughout the world, this hunger for the abundant life so very evident within all I've encountered. From the single mother, working tirelessly to provide for her child to the multimillionaire – the head of the company – and to the husband and wife seeking to maintain their happiness, we all share the deeply rooted desire for a much more abundant life.

I want to leave you with a word of encouragement and with what I believe to be, yet, another powerful principle in learning to master the Law of Creation within our daily lives: "When you are clear, the inspiration will flow." Oh, how I long to be a vessel of the power of the Spirit in the earth. I want the same for you. The moment that you allow yourself to become clear – free – from the limiting beliefs and old paradigms of yesteryear's indoctrination and the old system of belief, you will feel the force of inspiration beginning to flow through you as never before. When inspiration flows, with her will come the knowledge – the knowing – of not only what to think but also how to enact those thoughts by placing them into action. Inspiration will give you a definitive course of action.

As you become clear, the voice of the Spirit will not only become much more clear within your mind, but you will immediately and instantaneously begin to recognize that it has always, always been the Divine Mind operating through you the entire time. You will begin to see the greater and grander truth of the universe unfolding all around you. That you, yourself, have been the Creator all along, just as He designed.

About the Author

Dr. Jeremy Lopez is Founder and President of Identity Network International and Now Is Your Moment. Identity Network is one of the world's largest prophetic resource websites that reaches well over 153,000 people around the world and distributes books, audio teachings and DVDs. Jeremy has taught and prophesied to thousands of individuals worldwide from all walks of life, such as local church congregations, producers, investors, and various ministries throughout the world.

Dr. Jeremy Lopez is an international teacher, speaker, and dream coach who speaks on new dimensions of revelatory knowledge, mysteries, patterns, and cycles. He has a love for all people and desires to enrich their lives. This is accomplished through conferences, meetings, seminars, and various appearances on television and radio. He has coached and prophesied to, both, prime ministers and governors, including President Shimon Peres of Israel, Benjamin Natanyahu, and Governor Bob Riley of Alabama. He sits on various advisory boards worldwide.

Also By Jeremy Lopez

Abandoned to Divine Destiny

The Power of the Eternal Now

The Universe is at Your Command

Prophetic Transformation

Power Attraction

And many more